NO-BRAINER'S GUIDE TO WHAT CHR...

NO-BRAINER'S
GUIDE TO WHAT CHRISTIANS
BELIEVE

WRITTEN BY **JAMES S. BELL**, JR. AND **STAN CAMPBELL**

 TYNDALE HOUSE PUBLISHERS, INC., WHEATON, ILLINOIS

Visit Tyndale's exciting Web site at www.tyndale.com

Unless otherwise indicated, all Scripture quotations are taken from the *Holy Bible,* New Living Translation, copyright © 1996. Used by permission of Tyndale House Publishers, Inc., Wheaton, Illinois 60189. All rights reserved.

Scripture quotations marked NIV are taken from the *Holy Bible,* New International Version®. NIV®. Copyright © 1973, 1978, 1984 by International Bible Society. Used by permission of Zondervan Publishing House. All rights reserved.

Scripture quotations marked KJV are taken from the *Holy Bible,* King James Version.

Library of Congress Cataloging-in-Publication Data

Bell, James S.
  No-brainer's guide to what Christians believe / James S. Bell, Jr. and
Stan Campbell
      p. cm.
Includes bibliographical references.
  ISBN 0-8423-5596-0
  1. Theology, Doctrinal—Popular works. 2. Church history.
3. Christian ethics. I. Campbell, Stan. II. Title.
BT77 .B414 2002
230—dc21   2001008408

Printed in the United States of America

07 06 05 04 03 02
6   5   4   3   2   1

CONTENTS

PART IV:
EPILOGUE

"DON'T BE SILLY, COME ON OVER AND BRING THE KIDS. FRANK JUST OPENED UP A CAN OF WORMS."

Holy C.O.W. (Can of Worms)!

An Introduction to What Christians Believe

Every week, approximately 40 percent of the people in the United States leave their comfortable homes to attend a Christian church. (Considerably more are on the books as "Christian," but not all demonstrate it by church attendance.) Many go to Catholic Mass; others attend various Protestant groups. Most will go on Sunday; some prefer Saturdays or Wednesday nights. Some will sit quietly for an hour or so, listening to a rehearsed sermon; others won't be satisfied unless they are actively involved with singing, swaying, and vocal responses to the pastor's exhortations.

If you were to randomly drop in on half a dozen or so of the denominations that label themselves "Christian," you might have trouble figuring out what they could possibly have in common. A few continue to uphold Jewish holidays and traditions faithfully, while integrating Christian doctrine. Some are rigidly orthodox and formal. Some are so casual and low-key that you might think you've stumbled into a Sunday morning hootenanny rather than church.

SOME THINGS YOU'LL DISCOVER IN THIS CHAPTER

1. What to expect in this book

2. An explanation of the sidebars that will be used

3. Some challenges we'll need to confront in examining "what Christians believe"

1

So what do you expect from a book called the *No-Brainer's Guide to What Christians Believe?* Are you wondering which of these dozens of denominations sets the correct pattern for the rest of us to follow? Are you more interested in *doctrinal* definitions, or in the traditions and practices? Will this book guide you through the morass of who's right and who's wrong about every issue of what Christians believe? *Is* there one "right" way of doing things?

What to Expect

It won't take long to see that "what Christians believe" can be quite simple as long as we're speaking in broad generalities. The first section of this book will address some of the basic doctrines of the church that most, if not all, of Christendom will heartily endorse. We have come to some basic understandings about God, sin, salvation, and other teachings of Scripture. We may vary a bit as far as the details are concerned, but we can agree on the essentials. We'll try to determine what makes a congregation "Christian."

Yet as soon as we move into a lot of the specifics, the topic can quickly become a horrendous theological can of worms. So the second section of this book will deal with the obvious question: "Why don't all Christians believe the same things?" After all, didn't the church begin as a united cluster of believers? How did we go from being "all in one accord" to being an ever-increasing number of denominations and sub-denominations who don't seem to agree on much of anything? And is it a major problem and/or spiritual shortcoming not to be able to come to agreement more than we do?

We will see that, for a number of reasons, church splits have been taking place for almost two millennia now—some of them civil and others quite acrimonious. These days if you want to know "what Christians believe," the question soon becomes "*Which* Christians?" The faithful ones in the Roman Catholic Church who have retained much of the tradition and ceremony that has defined the church since its beginning? The spunky Protestants who protested their way out of favor with the established church of the time? The Puritans? The Pentecostals? Lutherans? Methodists? Southern Baptists? Missionary Baptists? General Baptists? Snake handlers?

It is a daunting assignment for a couple of writers to put pen to paper to attempt to describe "what Christians believe"—and to do so at a "no-brainer" level at that! It will not be the purpose of this book to address all the idiosyncrasies and distinctions of each and every variation of the Christian church. Space prevents it, as does the tolerance of the average reader. This book may include more than some people ever wanted to know, and it is likely to leave others frustrated that the topic wasn't pursued in more detail. If the former is true, you have our permission to skip ahead to a portion of the book you find more interesting. If the latter, be assured that other products exist that will go into gritty detail about every aspect of doctrine and church history. If you wish, you can spend the rest of your life studying "what Christians believe," and you'll probably never quite figure it out.

I Think I Need to See a Doctrine

You might think that with the Bible as an authority, with God exercising His will for His people and creation, and with the Holy Spirit actively involved in the lives of believers, all Christians would believe and act essentially the same way. When the total number of believers stood at a whopping 120 (before they had even acquired the name "Christians"), it was fairly easy to understand and explain what they believed (Acts 1:15). Jesus had just died, but the disciples were there to explain the significance of what had happened. The group was small enough to meet together for prayer and worship. They were hearing the same teachers, sharing the same meals, and interacting in natural ways.

But the church grew rapidly to 3,000 (Acts 2:41) and then to over 5,000 (Acts 4:4). Not long afterward, Christians in Jerusalem began to face persecution, and many of them scattered to various surrounding communities. As their geographic unity was disrupted, they began to be taught by different teachers and soon encountered some who didn't always have their best interests in mind. Many varying opinions were expressed in those early days, most of them using Scripture to some extent. For example, since Christianity grew out of Judaism, many of the first Jewish believers insisted that all Gentile believers be circumcised and otherwise become a bit more "Jewish." It wasn't a ludicrous request, because many Gentiles of the time were notorious for sin and promiscuity. And Old Testament law was clear about the importance of circumcision for anyone claiming to be one of God's people.

However, it was equally clear that God was beginning to work among the Gentiles as well as the Jews. And since the Holy Spirit was already active in the lives of non-Jewish believers, they wanted to know why they needed to endure circumcision and other Jewish traditions. This dilemma was the first debated by a church council, and the final ruling was that circumcision would not be required in order for someone to be a "Christian."

In this and many subsequent debates, a number of church-endorsed doctrines came to be included in the collection of "what Christians believe." While Scripture remained the authority, these doctrines were carefully interpreted and expressed with the insight of the apostles and other church leaders.

Not long after circumcision was forsaken as a requirement of acceptance into the church, the destruction of the temple did away with other traditional Jewish worship practices. In addition, the church was meeting on Sunday (the day of Jesus' resurrection) rather than Saturday, the Sabbath.

We will see that the advent of Jesus and the coming of the Holy Spirit initiated significant changes in what was perceived as proper worship of God. And frequently when a new doctrine was formulated and implemented—even though such doctrines were based on biblical teachings—the decision tended to divide the church according to the old way of thinking versus the new way. We will look at a number of these doctrinal controversies and other reasons why the church has divided and subdivided throughout the centuries.

Finally, a third section of this book will explore what Christians believe (and what perhaps tends to divide them) *today*. Believers in the twenty-first century face challenges and controversies unheard of in years past. How do we respond appropriately to advocates for gay rights, abortion, evolution, and so forth? Some Christians have a knee-jerk reaction to many such topics, yet they haven't done much to prepare themselves for a reasoned response to opponents. Again, a single book cannot do justice to all these hotly-debated issues, yet we will try to cover many of the basics and provide both sides of most of these crucial matters.

What's in the Margins?

As you read this book, you will see a number of recurring sidebars in the margins of the pages. We hope you'll find unusual and/or helpful information in these four types of sidebars that relate to the subject matter of the main text. The sidebars are as follows:

See for Yourself

We have said that most church doctrines and practices are based on the teachings of Scripture. This sidebar will point you to the source. Although we may occasionally get a bit overwhelmed by church history and/or dry doctrines, these sidebars will remind us why such things are important. In some cases the Scripture will be provided for you. In other cases, where the passage is longer than we can conveniently quote for you, we'll provide the reference and let you look it up yourself.

Questions?

Some books contain FAQs, or Frequently Asked Questions. But let's face it, when the topic is doctrine and church history, not a lot of questions are going to be *frequently* asked. Yet occasionally people raise questions on these topics that are relevant and interesting. We'll try to deal with such questions as we go through this book.

Says Who?

As we go from topic to topic throughout the book, we'll try to share some (we think) relevant quotes from other people with you. Naturally, when it comes to the doctrines and history of the church, you can expect some strong opinions.

Trivia Tidbit

This is a "catch all" category for interesting information. A Tidbit might be a big event in church history, a person you need to know about, a statistic that sheds light on the topic, or a number of other things.

We should also remind you that this book is one of a series. If your primary concern is what the Bible has to say or what you need to do to persevere in the Christian life, other titles in the series will be more relevant to your needs. There is also a book on the life of Jesus. But if you want to pursue the basic beliefs and doctrines of the Christian church, you're on your way.

You may be part of the 40 percent of the U. S. population who are weekly church attendees, or you may simply be curious to know what's going on behind those stained glass windows every Sunday. For whatever reason you picked up this book, we hope you find something helpful and relevant as we move ahead in our search for what Christians believe.

Questions to Ponder and/or Discuss

Look for this section at the end of each chapter. You'll find several questions to prompt more in-depth personal consideration. You can dwell on these questions privately if you wish. Or, if you are going through this book with a partner or small group, you can use them as discussion questions.

1. If you could speak to the absolute authority about "what Christians believe," what would be your top three questions?

2. If someone asked you right now, "What do the people at your church believe?" (and then went into specifics about

salvation, baptism, other religions, etc.) would you be able to answer with confidence? What grade would you give your answer?

3. How would you explain the basics of "what Christians believe" to the following people:

- A small child just learning about God and Jesus?
- A high school Sunday School class?
- A neighbor showing serious interest?
- A skeptical panel on *Politically Incorrect?*

Would your response in each case be pretty much the same, or would you vary your answers?

PART ONE

Doctrine, Doctrine, Give Me the News

"IT NEVER CEASES TO AMAZE ME HOW GREAT GOD REALLY IS. HE CREATED THE HEAVENS, THE EARTH, MAN AND ANIMALS. WHY, HE EVEN KNOWS THE NUMBER OF HAIRS ON YOUR HEAD. OK, SOME THINGS AREN'T AS DIFFICULT AS OTHERS, BUT HE'S STILL AMAZING."

The (Superhu)Man Upstairs

WHAT CHRISTIANS BELIEVE ABOUT GOD, JESUS, AND THE HOLY SPIRIT

In the beginning, God.

It was a good enough start for the Bible, so let's start at the same place as we begin to consider "what Christians believe." (After all, the beginning is usually a pretty good place to begin.)

All religions are based on a god of some kind, and Christianity is certainly no exception. The ancient Greeks and Romans had an entire cadre of gods and goddesses who were frequently perceived as a dysfunctional bunch, full of foibles and fury. When you think of Buddhism, perhaps the image that comes to mind is a god who might benefit from a little Slim-Fast. Ancient Norsemen associated thunder and lightning with the boomerang-like hammer of Thor, their war god. Other gods throughout the ages have been assigned images of fish, bulls, dogs, cats, birds, and many other animals. Sometimes human beings have set themselves up as gods. And many of these "gods" have collected quite a crowd of followers.

SOME THINGS YOU'LL DISCOVER IN THIS CHAPTER

1. The "Trinity" of God, and why we believe in one God rather than three

2. A list of some of the attributes of God

3. A reminder that God is always greater than our ability to figure Him out

11

God: Unlike Any Other

But the God worshiped by Christians stands apart from these other gods in a number of ways. To begin with, the Bible teaches that the Judeo-Christian God has *always* existed. Attempting to comprehend this concept can be very difficult for those of us who have always known cycles of time—day and night, summer and winter, birth and death. Yet the earliest chapters of Genesis tell us that these time limitations are creations of the eternal God. They are temporary restrictions, however, because we're also assured that ultimately we're destined for eternal life.

Using the line of reasoning that God has always existed, Judeo-Christian logic infers that any other so-called gods are actually idol-come-latelies. The preexistent God created *everything*, so if other gods appear at some point to compete with the original, they must have been made by people—not Him.

Another unique aspect of the capital-g God is that He has never encouraged the building of images in His honor—in fact, He forbids it. The first two of the Ten Commandments begin with a warning against worship of any other gods *as well as* a prohibition against even carving an image of a god (Exodus 20:3-4). While pagan temples were usually filled with various statues, portraits, and other artistic expressions of what their god(s) might look like, the first Jewish temple (or tabernacle, to be more precise) contained only a box to symbolize the presence of God. It was a special box, to be sure—the ark of the covenant was gold-plated and covered with a lid ("mercy seat") that portrayed two angels. Inside were a few prized souvenirs of Jewish history (see Hebrews 9:4). But by human standards, the ark of the covenant was certainly not on par with something like King Nebuchadnezzar's 90-foot-tall statue of gold (Daniel 3:1), the elaborate carvings of the rulers of Olympus around the top of the Parthenon, or other tributes to gods, goddesses, and demagogues throughout the ages.

The New Testament makes it clear that "God is spirit, so those who worship him must worship in spirit and in truth" (John 4:24). To think of God in the form of even the most magnificent animal—

whether fish, bull, elephant, or human—is to limit our comprehension of Him. The totality of God cannot be absorbed by the human mind, though we shouldn't stop trying. The crux of Christianity is that this infinite, complex Spirit who is God has reached out in love to a sinful, finite species of human beings, wanting to bond with them and draw them to Himself.

In trying to help us better understand who He is, God provided a written guidebook—the Bible. But many human beings resist homework and tend to go about the daily grind of life without looking to the Scriptures for help and direction.

God also sent people with special insight to tell others about him. The Old Testament prophets were ignored much more frequently than they were heeded. Many of today's pastors and teachers face the same problem as they attempt to communicate the reality of God to others. So after a considerable amount of time (at least in our human perspective), God sent "his only Son" (John 3:16).

Jesus: God within Reach

Jesus was sent to confirm everything that had been written about God, as well as what the prophets had said. And not only would He confirm those things, He would fulfill all the rest of the messianic prophecies that people were wondering about (Matthew 5:17-18). The birth of Jesus is described in the Gospel of John as something extraordinarily strange and special: "The Word [of God] became human and lived here on earth among us" (John 1:14). Jesus wouldn't just *say* all the right things; He could actually *show* us what God is like.

Jesus spent about 33 years on earth, but he was involved in public ministry for only three of them. He worked primarily among a dozen disciples to teach them and prepare them to carry on after He was gone. He got a lot of attention for His public miracles and healings and began to draw a crowd wherever He went. He also began to attract the attention and derision of the religious leaders of His time, who were threatened by the acclaim He received from the masses of people.

QUESTIONS?

Why was God represented by the ark of the covenant rather than some more personal image?

One of the primary differences between God and the idols of pagan religions is that God cannot be portrayed adequately by any single image. (This was one reason why the golden calf was such a big no-no; see Exodus 32.) Statues and idols suggested a familiarity that could never be assumed with the Judeo-Christian God. No matter how much a person knows about God, there is always much more that remains unknown. Therefore, the ark represented His presence, but not His person. Any other attempt to artistically portray God will come up far short. God is many things, but apparently He is not photogenic.

SAYS WHO?

"Who fathoms the Eternal Thought?
Who talks of scheme and plan?
The Lord is God! He needeth not
The poor device of man."
—*John Greenleaf Whittier*

13

SEE FOR YOURSELF
Belief in the divinity of Jesus marks a crucial distinction between Christianity and numerous other religions that believe He was a great guy—just not God. Many people attest that Jesus never really claimed to be God. But He did, and His claims were confirmed by those who knew Him best:

- An angel's confirmation of Jesus' divinity (Matthew 1:20-21; Luke 1:30-33)
- The disciples' confirmation (John 1:35-51; Matthew 16:13-20)
- God's confirmation (Mark 1:8-11)
- Jesus' own confirmations (John 4:25-26; 8:58; 10:30; 11:25-26; 14:6)

He eventually was convicted by a Roman court (fueled by accusations and misinformation from His opponents) and was crucified. The religious leaders knew Jesus had foretold His own resurrection, and they took every precaution to prevent it. The Gospels record their failure, because the resurrected Jesus was seen on no less than ten separate occasions before His final appearance when He ascended into heaven before the eyes of His disciples. (These events are documented in the *No-Brainer's Guide to Jesus*, so we won't go into further detail here.)

But among Jesus' final teachings was a promise that even though He would soon be returning to His Father, He would not leave His followers alone and helpless. He assured them of the coming of "another Counselor" (John 14:16).

The Holy Spirit: God within Us

The disciples didn't have to wait long for Jesus' promise to come true. About a week and a half after Jesus went up into heaven, the Holy Spirit came down at a gathering of believers with a sound "like the roaring of a mighty windstorm" and in the form of "what looked like flames or tongues of fire" (Acts 2:1-4). As a result, the believers found themselves speaking in other languages and were able to communicate the story of Jesus to various travelers in Jerusalem in the other peoples' native tongues. And from that point onward, the Holy Spirit is acknowledged as being instrumental in the growth and development of the church.

The Holy Spirit indwells each believer upon his or her confession of faith and belief in Jesus (Romans 5:5; 1 Corinthians 2:12). He (the Holy Spirit is described with the qualities of a *person* rather than merely those of a ghost or a force) assigns various "gifts" to believers that lend to the cohesion and effective operation of the church as the "body of Christ." The "fruit of the Spirit" is developed as believers yield to the direction of the Holy Spirit and discover genuine "love, joy, peace, patience, kindness, goodness, faithfulness, gentleness, and self-control" (Galatians 5:22-23).

The primary role of the Holy Spirit is to point to the significance of Jesus as Savior and Lord. The Holy Spirit draws nonbelievers to God (John 16:8-9) and accompanies each individual believer throughout a lifetime of learning and spiritual growth. He also acts as a kind of "interpreter" to ensure that God hears our pleas and prayers.

But just because the Holy Spirit is so prevalent throughout the New Testament doesn't mean He wasn't also around in the Old Testament as well. The "Spirit of God" is mentioned in regard to Creation (Genesis 1:2; Isaiah 40:12-13) and is said to have equipped certain individuals for specific tasks (such as Daniel [Daniel 5:11-12], Joshua [Numbers 27:18], Samson [Judges 15:14], and others). But in spite of numerous Old Testament references, the activity of the Holy Spirit among God's people was somewhat restricted until after the ministry and sacrifice of Jesus.

SEE FOR YOURSELF

"For we don't even know what we should pray for, nor how we should pray. But the Holy Spirit prays for us with groanings that cannot be expressed in words. And the Father who knows all hearts knows what the Spirit is saying, for the Spirit pleads for us believers in harmony with God's own will" (Romans 8:26-27).

When Math and Theology Don't Mix

God the Father. God the Son. God the Holy Spirit.

The Holy Trinity.

The Bible makes clear distinctions between the Father and the Son, the Father and the Spirit, and the Son and the Spirit. It doesn't take advanced math skills to add 1 + 1 + 1 and come up with three. Yet theologians tell us that's incorrect. God is one.

This concept of God is probably one of the most confusing for Christians to understand, much less explain to others. Yet we must try to comprehend this threefold description of the one God because it is foundational to what Christians believe as opposed to many other religions and cultic offshoots of Christianity.

Some people like to use a water analogy to try to clarify the confusion about the Holy Trinity. They say you can look at an iceberg, an expansive lake, and a geyser of hot steam. Each of these things has a distinct form unlike any of the others. Each is identifiable and unmistakable. Yet if you get down to the essence of each one, you would find identical molecules of H_2O. Other people rebut that the

SAYS WHO?

"It is curious to remark, that wherever the Holy Ghost is spoken of in the Bible, He is spoken of in terms of gentleness and love. We often read of 'the wrath of God' the Father, as Romans 1:18; and we read of the wrath of God the Son, as Psalms 2:12, but we nowhere read of the wrath of God the Holy Ghost."
—*Robert M. M'Cheyne*

SEE FOR YOURSELF

A couple of places in Scripture mention the three Persons of the Holy Trinity in regard to a singular purpose. The first was at Jesus' baptism, where Jesus stood in the water, God the Father spoke from heaven, and the Holy Spirit took the form of a dove and rested on Jesus (Matthew 3:16-17). The second is found in Jesus' "Great Commission" when He instructs His followers to make new disciples and baptize them "in the name of the Father and the Son and the Holy Spirit" (Matthew 28:19). These (and other) passages show that while each of the three Persons is God, God is also One.

complexity of God is hardly comparable to a basic science lesson about a simple molecule.

The Father, the Son, and the Holy Spirit are each clearly acknowledged as "God" in Scripture. And just as clear is the reminder that God is not just the *only* God, but He is a *single* God not to be confused with the plethora of Baals, Olympus figureheads, or other gods, where quantity sometimes seemed to outweigh any other significance.

The great three-in-one. Not three Gods, but one God in three distinct Persons. Not $1 + 1 + 1 = 3$, but $1 \times 1 \times 1 = 1$.

Who Could Ask for Anything More?

And since God is God, whether in the Person of the Father, the Son, or the Holy Spirit, any qualities attributed to one holy Person will be just as relevant to the other two. So let's take a look at some of the attributes of God, starting with the three "omnis" and going from there. (You may not find all the following *words* in Scripture, but the fundamental teachings about each of these beliefs are there.)

God is all-powerful (omnipotent)

When we think of almighty God, it doesn't always sink in that He is *all-mighty*. There is nothing He is incapable of doing, at least, nothing that is consistent with His character. Rookie philosophers sometimes ask, "Can God create a stone so large that even He can't lift it?" By posing such questions, they attempt to force a perceived weakness by limiting either God's creative power or His strength. But a more basic question is, "Why would God ever *want* to attempt something so foolish?" It would be like conducting research to see how many times you could hit yourself in the head with a hammer before giving yourself a concussion. It might be a fun bit of trivia in theory, but who *really* needs to know?

A better question is, "Why are there certain things that God can't (or won't) do?" For example, we are told that God cannot lie (Titus 1:2). He can't suddenly become unfaithful and break a promise or

16

covenant (2 Timothy 2:13). He can't tempt people to do something wrong, nor can He be tempted (James 1:13). Such actions are as contrary to the nature of God as creating universe-sized boulders simply to appease the whims of philosophical musers would be.

Rather than using wordplay to create an illusion that God's power is limited, perhaps we would do better to take a look at what God *can* do. He can create a habitable world by spinning an oxygen-covered rock around a fireball star without having it burn up or lose its gravitational pull and careen out into the vast expanse of the universe. He can generate new life among its people, plants, and animals through the miracle of reproduction. He can stroll there Himself, in human form, to turn water to wine, heal all sorts of diseases, walk on water, and even raise the dead. And He can provide love and eternal life for the people who live there, even though they rejected Him and *should* be allowed to die for their sins. All these things are miracles that only an omnipotent God can perform. And of course, there are many more.

SAYS WHO?

"It is impossible for that man to despair who remembers that his Helper is omnipotent."—*Jeremy Taylor*

God is everywhere (omnipresent)

Most of us know the frustration of spreading ourselves too thin when it comes to crucial relationships. A harried mom can do everything within her power to prepare supper for her husband while simultaneously talking to a close friend on the phone and personally attending to the spills and queries of two small children. But all those involved will be aware that they don't have the woman's full attention. The same goes for the most conscientious worker who simply has too many people to report to—none of the dozen bosses is likely to be satisfied with the person's performance.

God has no such restrictions of time and place. Wherever you are at any given moment, you have His full attention. So do the other six billion people on earth if they decide to seek Him at the same precise moment. When you get to the summit of Mount Everest, He'll be there waiting for you. When your bathyscaphe gets to the depths of the Marianas Trench in the Pacific Ocean, He'll be there as well.

Some philosophies attempt to remove the distinctions between the

QUESTIONS?

If indeed God is everywhere all the time, why does He "appear" to certain people?

On some occasions, God makes His presence known more clearly. For example, when the Israelites were being led out of Egypt, they always knew where to go because God went before them in a pillar of cloud by day and a pillar of fire by night. But just because He made His presence known out in front didn't mean He was unaware of what was going on at the back of the line. All of God is everywhere all the time. He is equally present whether He chooses to appear in a burning bush (Exodus 3:1-4), speak in "a gentle whisper" (1 Kings 19:11-13), or remain completely unseen and unheard.

Creator and His creation: God is in the trees, in the flowers, in the wind, and so forth. If you choose to sit in a tree or among the flowers on a windy day, you can find God there. But the presence of God is by no means restricted (or prorated) to any specific object or person.

God knows everything (omniscient)

As Creator and sustainer of all things, it only makes sense that God knows the tiniest intricacies of how everything functions. But taken to the extreme, that also means God never learns anything. He's never surprised or taken aback by events. He knows the punchline of every joke before the first word of it is spoken. He knows all of history, as well as the details of all future events. So when God leads or commands His people to do something, they shouldn't be so reluctant to obey. It's not like He's "playing the odds" for what is best for us. He *knows*!

When Job was going though his severe personal crises, he had a lot of questions about God's awareness of what he was experiencing. Finally, after a lot of doubts and confusion expressed by Job and his friends, God drilled Job with a series of questions of His own—covering everything from laying the foundations of the earth (Job 38:4) to what lies at the bottom of the seas (38:16) to the movements of the constellations (38:31-32) to the births of mountain goats (39:1) and much more. Job had been questioning God's awareness of one particular aspect of life. It's fascinating that God never (to our knowledge) gave Job the answers he requested, yet He made it clear that He knew much, much more than Job had even considered. Sometimes we need to be reminded that God knows more than we do.

God is sovereign

The United States has an "order of succession" with the President at the top and a well-thought-out series of people who would take charge in an emergency. Of all the possibilities for ruler of the universe, God is always sovereign—the top position on the list.

There is no chance that God will ever lose His number-one position, yet He is not a tyrant. He doesn't always demand His way. Jesus pointed people to God but allowed them to walk away when they didn't agree with His message or methods. Similarly, we still have the option of following God or not. People cause Him grief every day with their sin and rebellion. And when some choose to reject God, they create a lot of evil in the world that God gets blamed for.

One day, however, all the sin and rebellion will come to an end. In God's perfect, eternal kingdom, He will be the sovereign ruler—and no one will complain one bit!

God is righteous and holy

A common question is, "If God is sovereign, why does He allow suffering, evil, and other tragedies?" Someday God *will* completely do away with all imperfections, but in doing so He will have to judge and sentence all those who have rebelled against Him. Once that gavel falls, it's too late for excuses or a change of heart. So it is because of God's great patience that He extends the "sign-up period" for heaven, even though some of us may suffer in the meantime.

The concept of a "holy" God means He is "set apart" from any taint of sin or evil. Holiness implies separation. So not only is God righteous (completely just and fair) by nature, there is no possibility of His losing that righteousness. His holiness—His inability to be influenced by anything less than perfect—prevents Him from stumbling as we might. (We can learn from this that the better we separate our thoughts and behaviors from anything sinful or evil, the more righteousness we can experience as well.)

God is eternally unchanging and unchangeable

The big theological word for this characteristic is *immutable*. It simply means God is faithful, consistent, and can be counted on. In contrast with other gods of myth and legend, God doesn't act on one whim today and on another one tomorrow. People are sometimes fickle as they interact with God and one another, but God is constant. If He says He will do something, it will certainly be done.

God is love

In addition to everything so far, God is also perfectly loving. And God is not only *loving;* He is defined as *love* itself: "We know how much God loves us, and we have put our trust in him. God is love,

SEE FOR YOURSELF

"But you must not forget, dear friends, that a day is like a thousand years to the Lord, and a thousand years is like a day. The Lord isn't really being slow about his promise to return, as some people think. No, he is being patient for your sake. He does not want anyone to perish, so he is giving more time for everyone to repent. But the day of the Lord will come as unexpectedly as a thief. Then the heavens will pass away with a terrible noise, and everything in them will disappear in fire, and the earth and everything on it will be exposed to judgment" (2 Peter 3:8-10).

and all who live in love live in God, and God lives in them" (1 John 4:16).

The quality of love is thus elevated beyond a cute, Valentine's-Day feeling to something on par with ultimate power, all knowledge, holiness, eternity, and perfection itself. God relates to human beings in perfect love. When He gives us stuff, it is with perfect love. When He tries to turn us from potentially harmful thoughts and behaviors, He does so out of love. And one day He will judge the earth in all righteousness and love.

Only the Tip of the . . . *Elephant*?!

It's hard for the human mind to comprehend that God can be all these things (and more) simultaneously. If *you* were omnipotent and sovereign, would you reach out in love to people who had rejected and insulted you again and again? If you were all knowing, seeing clearly the sins of everyone else in the world, would you still care about anyone who couldn't approach your level of perfection? If people prayed to you and usually seemed much more focused on themselves than on you, how would you respond?

A classic story describes an outing by five blind men who encounter an elephant for the first time. Afterward, they all agree that it was a wonderful and fascinating experience. Yet that's about all they agree on. As the conversation continues, arguments break out between the five men.

The first man, who had felt the elephant's trunk, was convinced an elephant was much like a hose. The second disagreed, stating that an elephant was more like a wall (because he had approached the side of the great animal). The third man, who had happened to grab an ear, vehemently argued that the elephant was much like a fan. The fourth, after wrapping his arms around one of its legs, ridiculed his friends for not realizing the elephant was shaped like a tree. And the fifth, who had approached the animal from behind and had felt only its tail, swore that an elephant was more like a frayed rope than what any of his other friends were saying.

None of the five men doubted the existence—or even the magnifi-

cence—of elephants. Yet the argument to define and describe an "elephant" in more detail continued for years to come. After all, each had had a personal encounter and could not be swayed from his way of thinking.

And that's essentially how many of us approach our theology. We define God by our own personal encounters and are somewhat suspect of anyone else's. Yet God is infinitely larger than anyone's understanding of Him. We agree on certain aspects of God, as we have seen in this chapter, yet as future chapters will reveal, we tend to go our separate ways when someone gets a bit too insistent on one opinion over another.

One of us might cling to the compassionate, merciful, forgiving "piece" of God, and we might cling so tightly that we come to believe God would never send anyone to hell for eternity. Someone else might have suffered for a lifetime at the hands of evil men and women, persevering only by clinging to the righteousness "piece" of God that suggests He will not forever let the wicked go unpunished. Who is right? Perhaps both are, even though we can never fully comprehend it. The best we can do is keep searching for answers, ever pursuing additional clues to the totality of God.

Many things about God—whether speaking of the Father, Jesus the Son, or the Holy Spirit—must remain a mystery until He sees fit to reveal more of Himself to us. But that's okay. Mysteries can be fun. In the meantime we can look for clues and come up with a lot of the answers. But if you ever come across someone who claims to have *all* the answers, beware. Either he's still blind, or that's no elephant he has encountered.

TRIVIA TIDBIT

Chances are you've never heard of Timaeus of Locris, but perhaps you *have* heard of Voltaire. In attempting to describe God, Voltaire once quoted Timaeus' definition: "A circle whose center is everywhere and whose circumference is nowhere." (Just another illustration of how math and theology don't always mix.)

Questions to Ponder and/or Discuss

1. What are some of the "nicknames" you've heard that are used in reference to God ("the man upstairs," "the big guy," etc.)? Does the use of such casual terms bother you? Why or why not?

2. Which of the attributes of God are most important to you personally in your current conditions in life? Which do you usually tend to downplay or overlook?

3. On a scale of 1 (least) to 10 (most), how well do you think you understand the basics about:

God the Father?   1   2   3   4   5   6   7   8   9   10

Jesus?   1   2   3   4   5   6   7   8   9   10

The Holy Spirit?   1   2   3   4   5   6   7   8   9   10

4. Does it frustrate you not to know *everything*, or do you relish pursuing the ongoing mystery of the nature of God?

"HI, WE'RE WITH CITIZENS UTILITIES AND WE'D LIKE TO MEET WITH PASTOR BURNS. WE UNDERSTAND HE'S GOT ACCESS TO AN UNLIMITED FREE POWER SOURCE."

CHAPTER THREE

Powers That Be

SATAN, ANGELS, DEMONS, HEAVEN, AND HELL

He holds the title of prince. You sometimes have to give him his due, or perhaps you'll be called on to play his advocate. Speak of him, and he may appear. He once debated Daniel Webster. Later he went down to Georgia, "lookin' for a soul to steal." He's on cans of Armour luncheon meat. Flip Wilson used to blame him for a lot of misbehavior.

He is, of course, the devil. Satan. The Prince of Darkness. Lucifer. Beelzebub. Mephistopheles. Old Scratch. The foul fiend. The cloven hoof. Perhaps you know him by other names as well.

He has a number of titles and descriptions, and stories about the devil are abundant. In fact, we may have formed more opinions about him based on legends and other portrayals than what we know for sure about him from the Bible. We may tend to perceive him as a comic figure in a cheesy red cape holding a pitchfork (à la Saturday Night Live). We may even be encouraged to take pity on him as a misunderstood underdog destined always to be one-upped by the God he rebelled against.

SOME THINGS YOU'LL DISCOVER IN THIS CHAPTER

1. A best guess as to how Satan and evil came to be

2. A comparison of biblical and popular/traditional perspectives of Satan and angels

3. Warnings about hell and promises about heaven

23

TRIVIA TIDBIT

Artistic portrayals of the devil frequently show him with cloven hooves. This originated in old Rabbinical writings where he is called *seirizzim* (a goat). Anything with a cloven hoof was considered unclean to the Old Testament people of God, and the devil became the ultimate figurehead for evil and uncleanness—down to the tips of his hooves.

SAYS WHO?

"Wherever God erects a house of prayer,
The devil always builds a chapel there;
And 'twill be found, upon examination,
The latter has the largest congregation."
—*Daniel Defoe*

Or perhaps you've experienced the other extreme. Some of the more notable horror movies portray the devil as an adversary who cannot be overcome without the help of secret knowledge, a long-lost ancient incantation, or a hulking Hollywood leading man. Otherwise, people are powerless to resist him.

In this chapter we want to take a look at our *adversary* and *accuser* (which is what the words "Satan" and "devil" mean). And in connection with this primary adversary, we'll look at some of his peers—angels and demons. We'll start with what we can find in the Bible, and then we'll look at some beliefs common to many Christians that are built on those biblical basics.

Just Call Me Angel of the Morning Star

We said in the last chapter that God is eternal—that He has always existed. We also said that another of His qualities is perfect love. Christians believe that at some point in time, perhaps long before the creation of human beings, God created angels with whom He could interact. He could bestow His love on them, and they were free to return that love. And since another of God's attributes is holiness, the angels would have to be holy as well to remain in His presence.

The being we know as Satan began as an angel—a high-ranking angel, if not number one among the angelic army. He is sometimes referred to as Lucifer, a Latin term meaning "morning star" (Isaiah 14:12). Since God was his creator, we know he was perfect. And *he* knew it as well.

There's nothing wrong with looking in a mirror and thinking, "What a magnificent creation of God I am!"—as long as all credit (and no blame) is assigned to the Creator, who has the unbreakable copyright/trademark on your body, soul, mind, and spirit. But apparently the "morning star" used his God-given freedom of choice to begin to think so highly of himself that he eventually rebelled against God. Pride is a tricky emotion—a little is healthy (in light of being created in the image of God), but too much has a dark and twisted effect. The devil became so proud that he wanted to be even greater than God Himself.

After the devil rebelled against God, he lost his backstage pass to heaven and was cast out of God's presence. He went from being Lucifer ("morning star") to Satan ("adversary"). Jesus told His disciples, "I saw Satan falling from heaven as a flash of lightning!" (Luke 10:18), though He didn't elaborate on the statement. And while God could have destroyed the devil then and there, God determined to delay his ultimate demise. For the time being, Satan was allowed to go "back and forth across the earth, watching everything that's going on" (Job 1:7). He apparently has occasional contact with God, but he is *persona non grata* in the heavenly realms.

As soon as God majestically reached out to create the world as we know it and peopled it with beings who could interact with Him and receive His love, the devil was there. Since God and Satan were enemies, any potential friend of God immediately became a target for the devil. So taking the form of a serpent, he conned Adam and Eve out of Paradise (Genesis 3). God had created the idyllic setting of Eden where He could get up close and personal with His beloved human beings, but Satan quickly undermined the deal, severing the close bond between humanity and God and sending people out of Paradise and into the weed fields to scrape out a living.

From that point forward, sin was the rule rather than the exception. Satan's continued influence over people is well documented in Scripture. In response to God's efforts to restore a workable (though no longer perfect) connection with people through written commandments, sacrifices, prophets, judges, kings, and other means, Satan twisted God's words, tempted God's followers, and led many people astray. He still does.

QUESTIONS?

Did God create angels and people because He was lonely?

God is complete in every way. To imply loneliness is to suggest a lack of self-satisfaction and/or a need for a companion. God neither lacks nor needs anything. However, since love is a quality that works by involving others, and since God is love, He graciously invites others to share His existence. For example, you might be sitting around with three friends having a wonderful time and in want of nothing. But if a fourth close friend were to join you, it would be that much better. God initiated a wider "circle of friends," not out of need or loneliness, but out of love.

Satanic Name Calling

Satan's negative influence has led to his acquiring a number of names and titles. Below are just a few:

- "The father of lies" (John 8:44)

SEE FOR YOURSELF

Isaiah 14:12-17; Ezekiel 28:12-19

The account of how the devil fell and sin started is one of those strongly debated issues. These two biblical passages provide a convincing argument for some scholars; others disagree completely. Both passages are addressed to a specific individual, yet, as is the case with many prophecies, there may indeed be a twofold meaning—one that applies to the human leaders and a second, more cryptic interpretation.

If we rule out these passages as applying to Satan, essentially all we know about the devil's pre-Eden existence is, "He was a murderer from the beginning and has always hated the truth. There is no truth in him" (John 8:44).

- "The god of this evil world" (2 Corinthians 4:4)
- "The mighty prince of the power of the air" (Ephesians 2:2)
- The "great dragon" (Revelation 12:9)
- "The ancient serpent called the devil" (Revelation 12:9)
- "The Accuser" (Revelation 12:10)

From Adam and Eve to the most recent birth at your local hospital, the devil has placed his mark on humanity. And you can count on Satan attempting to maneuver his way into each and every person's life through that "loophole" of freedom of choice. From the debacle at Eden to the wickedness of Sodom and Gomorrah to massive idolatry and Baal worship to false teachers and doctrines, Satan has been quite a busy little imp over the centuries.

Satan, though he is the essence of evil, is no dummy. Eve didn't see a squatty little red figure poking her with a trident. She saw a beautiful animal promising her greater insight if she went against God's clear instructions and listened to Satan's silver (though forked) tongue instead. Throughout history, the devil has borne out what Paul revealed about him: "Even Satan can disguise himself as an angel of light" (2 Corinthians 11:14). The devil inspires "false messiahs and false prophets [who] will rise up and perform great miraculous signs and wonders so as to deceive, if possible, even God's chosen ones" (Matthew 24:24).

When Satan approaches, we never see the horns or the sneer. We see a well-practiced smile and hear the promise of great truth that will prove to be half-truth at best. The devil is crafty, so we usually see what we *want* to see. And we waste our God-given gift of freedom of choice to chase selfish, sinful pursuits rather than godly ones. Many times much harm has been done by the time we discover that we've been hustled.

But for all his manic devotion to opposing God, the devil has his limits. He is not omnipotent, omniscient, or omnipresent. In order to work at a worldwide level, he had to recruit an army of his own, giving rise to yet another title: "the prince of demons" (Matthew 9:34).

While people today tend to scoff or dispute the existence of demons, the Bible clearly acknowledges their existence and influ-

ence. What isn't exactly clear is what demons are. A good case can be made that they are fallen angels, who supported Satan in his rebellion against God and continue to work for him. Other explanations throughout the ages have suggested that demons are the spirits of evil people who have died, spirits of people who existed prior to Adam who roam the earth seeking bodies to possess, or even the offspring produced when the "sons of God" mated with the "beautiful women of the human race" (Genesis 6:2). Good biblical arguments can be made to refute these speculations, so the consideration that demons are fallen angels remains the best option.

So before we look at the fallen angels who possibly rebelled (with Satan) against God, let's see what we can discover about angels in general.

How Many Angels Can Dance on the Shelf of a Bookstore?

There was a time when not much was written about angels. But with the recent increase in curiosity about spirituality and religion (not necessarily Christian), angels have become profit centers. They have their own calendars, are popular as figurines, and have been quite successful in their own television series. While the general public may oppose many of the teachings of the Bible, they don't seem to mind the possibility of angels hanging around.

Yet the biblical description of angels is very different from both the young-and-chubby-cherub and sleek-and-sexy-vixen varieties of angels so frequently portrayed. The appearance of angels throughout Scripture almost always inspired fear and trembling among those who witnessed their arrival. Though neither omnipotent nor omniscient, angels exhibit tremendous power and high intelligence, not to mention their behind-the-scenes knowledge of what's happening in heaven.

We don't know exactly when they were created, but we are told angels were around to witness the creation of the earth (Job 38:4-7). Unlike the way He created people, God didn't create a couple of

QUESTIONS?

Why does God allow Satan's activity to go unchecked?

As active and influential as the devil is in our world, God limits his control. God, in His infinite wisdom, allows Satan to recruit followers from among us human beings. While God has done everything possible to prove His love for us, and while He urges us to follow Him and experience all the benefits He offers, He also allows us the freedom to reject Him if we so desire.

SEE FOR YOURSELF

"Remember that the temptations that come into your life are no different from what others experience. And God is faithful. He will keep the temptation from becoming so strong that you can't stand up against it. When you are tempted, he will show you a way out so that you will not give in to it . . . " (1 Corinthians 10:13).

SEE FOR YOURSELF

"Be careful! Watch out for attacks from the devil, your great enemy. He prowls around like a roaring lion, looking for some victim to devour. Take a firm stand against him, and be strong in your faith" (1 Peter 5:8-9).

SAYS WHO?

"It is so stupid of modern civilization to have given up believing in the devil when he is the only explanation of it."
—Ronald Knox

angels and let them multiply. They are a not a "race," as such, yet they comprise quite a multitude. In John's vision, he saw "thousands and millions" of them (Revelation 5:11).

Yet of all the angels that populate the heavenly realms, only two are mentioned by name in the Bible. (Apocryphal literature numbers the archangels at seven and provides a few additional names.) One primary figure, an archangel, is named Michael (Jude 9). Another prominent angel is Gabriel, who appeared to Daniel (Daniel 8:16) and was later privileged to announce the upcoming births of both John the Baptist (Luke 1:11-20) and Jesus (Luke 1:26-38).

The Bible suggests that angels are grouped into certain ranks, though the flowchart of the angelic chain of command is debatable. Some of the rankings include archangels, "chief princes" or "spirit princes" (Daniel 10:13), cherubim (Ezekiel 28:14-16, NIV), and seraphim (Isaiah 6:2, 6). Other titles used to denote angels are "principalities," "powers," "thrones," "dominions," and a few others, depending on your translation. Some of the more current Bible paraphrases attempt to simplify this potentially confusing heavenly power structure by referring to "mighty angelic guardians" rather than using so many specific terms.

When angels are described in the heavens, they are usually praising God. They serve as messengers to communicate important messages from God to people. We know they were especially active in the life, ministry, death, and resurrection of Jesus. They also played key roles in the lives of Abraham, Jacob, Daniel, Balaam, Peter, and other biblical characters. The Bible doesn't speak of "guardian angels," as such, but the idea that each person has an angel overseer assigned to him or her may come from Jesus' statement: "Beware that you don't despise a single one of these little [children]. For I tell you that in heaven their angels are always in the presence of my heavenly Father" (Matthew 18:10).

When Good Angels Go Bad

Biblical details are sketchy, but we know that at some point, a number of God's holy, created angels chose to rebel against Him. We frequently refer to this group as "fallen angels." It is also assumed that these are the forces that became the "demons" or "evil spirits" mentioned throughout Scripture. For some reason, part of this group of devil-supporting angels was allowed to go about their work in opposing God and His people.

Jesus and the early apostles are cited as casting out a number of such evil spirits. The demons could demonstrate great power over certain people, causing blindness, deafness, mental instability, physical self-harm, and more kinds of damage. Yet Jesus demonstrated complete authority over the evil spirits. Even before He had said much about who He really was, they identified Him as "Jesus, Son of the Most High God" (Mark 5:7). They even asked for a favor (Mark 5:12), indicating their submission to Him. Throughout the Gospels, every time Jesus commanded an evil spirit to do something, it obeyed—no matter how much influence it had exhibited over someone else.

We learn a bit more about evil spirits from other New Testament writers. Demons can initiate "lying spirits and teachings" which lead people away from God's clear truth (1 Timothy 4:1). And at an even more basic level, they attempt to obscure the importance of Jesus in regard to people's faith (1 John 4:1-4). Though they have no influence over Jesus, they can still make headway among God's people by undermining the truth of biblical doctrines.

And these are just the evil spirits who have, for some reason, been allowed to exert an influence in the world. They are well aware, however, that their days are numbered. The future holds "God's appointed time" for their power to come to an end (Matthew 8:29).

Other fallen angels, however, were *not* allowed the freedom to torment people. Instead, they were imprisoned (2 Peter 2:4; Jude 6). Their future doom in the lake of eternal fire is assured (Matthew 25:41), but they haven't yet been sentenced in the final act of God's judgment. In fact, the book of Revelation prophesies heavy demonic activity in the last days. During this period, some of the most ferocious of the demons will be released from the "bottomless pit" or "abyss" to work for a while until God ultimately destroys them all

TRIVIA TIDBIT

A popular plot line is that people become angels when they die, but it is by no means biblical. People and angels are on different spiritual planes. Humans are created "lower than the angels" (Psalm 8:4-6; Hebrews 2:6-8, KJV). So when Jesus became human, He took quite a demotion from being "supreme over all creation" (Colossians 1:15). Yet thanks to His sacrificial act, believers receive the status of "God's children," and when they die they are entitled to "everything God gives to his Son, Christ" (Romans 8:16-17). With so much to look forward to, who would want to settle for being an angel?

SAYS WHO?

"But all God's angels come to us disguised:
Sorrow and sickness, poverty and death,
One after other lift their frowning masks,
And we behold the Seraph's face beneath,
All radiant with the glory and the calm
Of having looked upon the front of God."
—J. R. Lowell

SAYS WHO?

"Oftentimes, to win us to our harm,
The instruments of darkness tell us
truths;
Win us with honest trifles, to betray's
In deepest consequence."
—William Shakespeare

TRIVIA TIDBIT

According to the Koran, hell has seven
portals, each leading to a different
section. Buddhism doesn't deal with hell
as such, yet it speaks of as many as 136
places where the dead will be punished.

(Revelation 9:1-3, 11; 11:7; 17:8). The king of this merciless bunch is known as *Abaddon* (Hebrew) or *Apollyon* (Greek), which means "Destroyer." Even Satan will be imprisoned in the bottomless pit for a time prior to his final judgment (Revelation 20:1-3).

Raising Hell (As a Topic for Discussion, That Is)

A number of cartoons, comedy skits, and other sources portray the devil and his minions as rulers in hell, where they get great satisfaction from torturing the souls of humans they have lured there. But nowhere does the Bible give us that impression.

In fact, we are told that hell is a terrifying place prepared especially for the judgment of the devil and his followers (Matthew 25:41). It is not a separate kingdom ruled by Satan and staffed with authoritative demons; it is a place of final punishment. In John's vision in Revelation, he witnesses the Antichrist and false prophet, as well as Satan himself, judged by God and tossed alive into "the lake of fire that burns with sulfur" where "they will be tormented day and night forever and ever" (Revelation 19:20; 20:10).

However, hell has also become the final destination for *people* who reject God. Satan's followers will share in Satan's judgment. Hell isn't usually a favorite topic of discussion, because we don't like to believe that God would actually tell someone, "No, you can't spend eternity with Me. Go instead to a horrendous, fiery, eternal doom." What happened to His love and compassion?

Yet another of God's titles is that of *judge*. Our court systems are filled with loving and compassionate judges who, in order to be fair and just, must sentence offenders in ways they might not prefer to. Young children are sent to juvenile homes. Fathers are separated from wives and families to do time behind bars and barbwired walls. Some people are even sentenced to die. And in each of these cases, the ruling of the judge has very little to do with his or her love and compassion. In fact, some of these rulings may be a compassionate response to the *victims* involved.

We should keep in mind that most of the factual information we have about hell came from no less an authority than Jesus Himself.

He not only included the topic in His straightforward teachings and warnings, but He also made numerous references in His stories (Luke 16:19-31). A number of His parables end with "weeping and gnashing of teeth" and/or "eternal punishment" (Matthew 24:51; 25:30; 25:46; etc.). Jesus didn't pull any punches or soft-pedal this crucial topic. He spoke of unquenchable fire (Matthew 18:8) and "anguish in these flames" (Luke 16:24), and He warned His followers to avoid hell no matter what the cost (Matthew 18:7-9).

However, this is a topic where Christians disagree. Some denominations teach that hell is a truly terrible place where God sentences unrepentant sinners, but not one of *eternal* punishment. Others promote the concept of *purgatory*, a place where souls suffer only until purged from sin. And other explanations are available as well.

In any event, to dwell too heavily on the terrors of hell is to get the spiritual cart before the horse. The primary message of Jesus was expressed in much more positive terms: "God so loved the world that he gave his only Son, so that everyone who believes in him will not perish but have eternal life. God did not send his Son into the world to condemn it, but to save it. There is no judgment awaiting those who trust him" (John 3:16-18).

We can rest assured that God doesn't desire for anyone to go to hell. Jesus is the perfect sacrifice for sin, and God is the perfect judge. There will be no mistakes. No one will stumble into hell and suffer forever because of a clerical error, an inept attorney, or any other "accident."

SEE FOR YOURSELF

"So you see, the Lord knows how to rescue godly people from their trials, even while punishing the wicked right up until the day of judgment. He is especially hard on those who follow their own evil, lustful desires and who despise authority. . . . The Lord isn't really being slow about his promise to return, as some people think. No, he is being patient for your sake. He does not want anyone to perish, so he is giving more time for everyone to repent" (2 Peter 2:9-10; 3:9).

Going Up?

Just as God has prepared a place for the devil and his followers, He has also prepared a place for those who follow Him. One of Jesus' last promises to His disciples was this: "Don't be troubled. You trust God, now trust in me. There are many rooms in my Father's home, and I am going to prepare a place for you. If this were not so, I would tell you plainly. When everything is ready, I will come and get you, so that you will always be with me where I am" (John 14:1-3).

Just as the Bible gives a no-holds-barred description of the agonies of hell, it also provides a breathtaking account of heaven. Paul speaks of being called into "the third heaven" where he "heard things so astounding that they cannot be told" (2 Corinthians 12:2-4). John also witnessed grand images of God's heavenly city in his revelation. Streets of gold? Check. Pearly gates? You betcha! No more sorrow, fears, sin, or pain. God will wipe every tear from every eye.

But forget the gold, gems, harps, and crowns. The best part of eternity in heaven will be the reconnection of people with God as He originally intended it. With sin disposed of, nothing stands between you and your Creator. You no longer need to fear Him as a judge. You can embrace Him as a child hugs a parent.

Envisioning the Invisible

Although we can't see them, we are surrounded by a number of powers. Indeed, Paul reminds us that we shouldn't be so quick to fight and bicker with one another, because that's a waste of effort and energy. He writes: "For we are not fighting against people made of flesh and blood, but against the evil rulers and authorities of the unseen world, against those mighty powers of darkness who rule this world, and against wicked spirits in the heavenly realms" (Ephesians 6:12).

Just because our spiritual enemies are unseen doesn't mean they aren't real. The devil and his armies are hard at work in our world, and it's more than a game to them. Satan is a prowling lion looking for another meal (1 Peter 5:8), but he is disguised as an angel of light (2 Corinthians 11:14).

So as we saw in the last chapter, Christians believe that God, Jesus, and the Holy Spirit are one and are active in running things and in seeking our love. At the same time, the devil and a horde of evil supporters are also at work. With these things in mind, where does that leave *us*? We'll see how we humans fit into the picture in the next chapter.

Questions to Ponder and/or Discuss

1. How many books/movies can you think of with satanic/demonic themes? How would you explain the phenomenal success and acceptance of such things in our society?

2. How did you learn about Satan, angels, heaven, and hell? How does what you've learned stack up against biblical doctrine?

3. Why do you think Scripture has so much to say about these unseen forces? If "ignorance is bliss," wouldn't it be easier for us to remain in the dark rather than develop a curiosity about invisible things?

CHAPTER FOUR

"GRANTED, LYLE, WE'RE NOT THE SMARTEST ANIMALS IN THE WORLD, BUT WHY DO HUMANS MAKE SALVATION SO DIFFICULT? CHRIST DIED FOR THEIR SINS. HE LEADS, THEY FOLLOW."

Between the Rock and a Hot Place

ESSENTIAL ASPECTS OF SALVATION

Perhaps you've found yourself in a position where two of your friends or relatives are feuding, and the conflict seems to keep escalating. With time, each of the parties is likely to seek your support, and you'll find it impossible to remain friends with one of them without offending the other. Magnify this situation by a couple of million levels of intensity, and you begin to understand where you are in the conflict between God and Satan. Satan's rebellion took place before time as we know it, and it will continue until it is ultimately put to an end. In the meantime, as a human being, you're caught in the middle. Both parties are calling for your loyalty.

Ceased of Eden

Yet we are not mere pawns in the ongoing clash between good and evil, God and the devil. When God created human beings to throw into the mix, He made clear a number of things. Among them, He was our ally. He knew what was best for us. He loved us and desired

SOME THINGS YOU'LL DISCOVER IN THIS CHAPTER

1. The uniqueness of God's plan of salvation for humanity

2. How to overcome "natural" limitations

3. A list of spiritual benefits God provides each believer

QUESTIONS?

Wasn't placing the "tree of the knowledge of good and evil" (Genesis 2:15-17) in Eden a cruel joke, akin to dangling a piece of candy in front of a child and then slapping his hand every time he reaches for it?

Some people have tried to make this case. But others insist that this was God's way of giving His new creations free will, freedom of choice. Had He not included that single off-limits tree among all the others, Adam and Eve couldn't have chosen *not* to obey God. They would have been little more than flesh-and-blood computers programmed to perform certain functions while avoiding others. Instead, God shared His will with them and allowed them to decide whether or not to adhere to it. People find themselves with that same choice today.

SAYS WHO?

"Salvation is . . . bringing back to normal, the Creator-creature relation."
—A. W. Tozer

our love in return. He provided a paradise free from sin, guilt, and shame. And yet He included one tree among the orchards of Eden that was off-limits, making it clear that eating of this tree would lead to death. He gave the first humans a clear choice: obey Him or not.

Free will got the first human beings in trouble because they chose poorly. Yet it's that same freedom of choice that allows people today, if they so desire, to approach God again and restore the bond that sin has broken. This is one way that Christianity differs from other religions. We believe God is ultimately in control of all world events. Therefore, an intentional decision to follow and obey Him results in definite benefits—some more long-range than others, but sure and certain benefits all the same.

Christians reject the concept of karma, with its everything-averages-out-in-the-end philosophy, in favor of a belief that God's will is going to be accomplished in His way and in His time. In the meantime, He is overseeing everything and will reward the righteous while judging the wicked.

Christians also reject the concept of reincarnation, which suggests we keep coming back until we get it right, for the belief that God is able to coach us through and get it right the first time—not in *our* power, but in His. And where most belief systems place the onus on us to perform to a certain standard before being accepted and rewarded by the deity of choice, the Christian God has initiated the redemptive process and has issued an invitation to anyone and everyone interested in an eternal, loving relationship. All that is required for entrance into His kingdom is a repentant heart and belief in His Son as Lord and Savior.

In light of such news, and in response to such a wonderful and free gift, we are expected to cast aside our wicked ways and begin to do "good works" for God. Yet without faith in Jesus to begin with, no amount of work will "earn" God's kingdom for us.

It's sin that separates us from God, not merely laziness. God is the only one who can deal with the sin problem, and if we don't follow His clear instructions, we have no other options. Spiritual lethargy is a serious problem, too, but a genuine relationship with God usually solves that little problem. When we quit trying to work our way to God and instead use our energy to *respond* to all He has done for us, we find ourselves more motivated than ever.

Christianity: Doing What Comes Unnaturally

Still, throughout our lives we are caught in the spiritual tension that exists between God and Satan. It may feel as if you're the center of a supernatural tug-of-war at times. But more accurately, you're only being recruited by two different armies. You choose one or the other, and then learn to deal with the choice you have made.

Because Adam and Eve's sin has been passed down to everyone born since, it's a depressing fact that we start out in Satan's ranks. Satan has earned his title "god [or prince] of this world" (John 12:31; 2 Corinthians 4:4). In a world corrupted by sin, this is no surprise, since he is the one who originated sin even before the creation of the earth.

When we go with our basic instincts we may find ourselves involved in any number of sins. Something feels *natural* about sin. We may even justify a number of favorite sins by claiming it's just our human *nature*. And we may be familiar with one or more of the "desires of the sinful nature" listed in Galatians 5:19-21: sexual immorality, impure thoughts, eagerness for lustful pleasure, idolatry, participation in demonic activities, hostility, quarreling, jealousy, outbursts of anger, selfish ambition, divisions, the feeling that everyone is wrong except those in your own little group, envy, drunkenness, wild parties, and other kinds of sin. When we find ourselves involved in these kinds of things, we feel just like most of the other people we know.

Yet even though such thoughts and actions may feel natural, they usually don't feel quite *right*. People are created in the image of God, and sin separates us from Him. During the creation process God said, "Let us make people in our image, to be like ourselves" (Genesis 1:26). Theologians debate what, exactly, it means to be "in God's image." But many agree this means that we were created with a will, with emotions, with intelligence, and with a spiritual aspect and purpose that goes far beyond merely a physical body

SEE FOR YOURSELF

When the Bible refers to the "natural" person, it is the sinful, imperfect part of us. The King James Version made more references to the "natural" man than some of the newer translations. For example, consider 1 Corinthians 2:14: "But the natural man receiveth not the things of the Spirit of God; for they are foolishness unto him, neither can he know them, because they are spiritually discerned." The definition of "natural man" is clear, even in King James language. But more recent translations of "natural man" include "the man without the Spirit" (NIV) and "people who aren't Christians" (NLT).

TRIVIA TIDBIT

Certain scholars of the Talmud have suggested that Adam was in Eden as little as twelve hours before being cast out. Other people speculate it could have been decades or centuries before he and Eve succumbed to the serpent's temptation.

SAYS WHO?

"No man knows how bad he is until he has tried to be good. There is a silly idea . . . that good people don't know what temptation means."—*C. S. Lewis*

and temporary existence. We are similar to other animals in regard to life and death, flesh and blood, and even brains and behaviors. But we are uniquely in God's image when soul and spirit come into play.

I'm Fallen and I Can't Get Up

In the beginning, humans and God were united in will and purpose. It was possible to walk with God and know Him in an intimate way. But then came the fall of Adam and Eve, and we have been fallen ever since. Now God seems distant, remote, and mysterious. Yet we have retained His image to a great degree, and our soul and spirit feel a void and a need to reconnect.

So when it comes to everyday life, the natural person seeks wealth, comfort, and self-satisfaction. And if the pursuit of such things is motivated by greed and leads to stepping all over other people to get them, so be it. Our natural urges are strong.

But some people realize there is more to life than those basic natural desires. They too might *want* to be healthy, wealthy, and self-actualized. But the wealth and/or other benefits just aren't worth it if they come at the expense of another person's feelings, the destruction of an animal species, the ruination of a rainforest, or a similar drastic toll. This group of people probably feel the same natural drives and desires, yet they also are in tune somewhat with the godly mold into which they have been cast. As God calls them to higher goals and standards, He also shows them the remedy for the sin barrier that separates them from Him.

And that's where that old free will comes in. We can choose to remain on the selfish, natural (bottom) rung of the ladder, or we can respond to God's gracious invitation to go higher.

In the supernatural struggle going on around us, our choice of whom to support will have eternal consequences. It's not like the devil doesn't have a lot to offer. He even tried to secure Jesus' loyalty by promising Him "the nations of the world and all their glory" (Matthew 4:8-9). A lot of us settle for much less. But Jesus wisely quoted a relevant Scripture and told Satan to get lost. The devil's temptations are never quite as attractive when we realize God always has much, much more to offer.

Who Could Ask for Anything More?

So let's look at a few of the things God offers people as they consider whom to follow. The following is a list of doctrinal terms beginning with *salvation* and moving on to related issues. Whether or not we realize it, and whether or not we even care, a lot of official/legal/spiritual things take place whenever a person places his or her faith and loyalty in Jesus. We speak of simple faith, and it is—as far as *we're* concerned. But on God's end of the bargain, His ability to forgive and accept us is more complicated.

Salvation

Salvation is one of the crucial doctrines of the Christian faith. At its most basic level, the theological concept of salvation is not unlike any situation today where one person is drowning, hanging from a cliff, or in some other precarious circumstance when another person shows up and saves him or her.

Scripture makes clear that "all have sinned" (Romans 3:23) and that "the wages of sin is death" (Romans 6:23). Unless something or someone intervenes, we're goners . . . spiritual toast in a horrendous eternal toaster.

Yet God has stepped into this critical situation to save our lives. We were going to die for sure, but God appeared on the scene and made sure it didn't have to happen. That's salvation. That's at the core of most other doctrines of the faith.

Grace

Grace is related to salvation. When we begin to ask *why* God would step in to save us if it required the death of Jesus, we don't come up with many good answers. We rejected His original plan, remember? And it's not like we're good people at heart, because at heart we're those nasty, self-centered, sinful little sons (and daughters) of the devil.

So "grace" is defined as "undeserved favor." We did nothing—no

SEE FOR YOURSELF

"When we were utterly helpless, Christ came at just the right time and died for us sinners. . . . God showed his great love for us by sending Christ to die for us while we were still sinners. And since we have been made right in God's sight by the blood of Christ, he will certainly save us from God's judgment. . . . So now we can rejoice in our wonderful new relationship with God—all because of what our Lord Jesus Christ has done for us in making us friends of God" (portions of Romans 5:6-11).

SAYS WHO?

"The quality of mercy is not strain'd; it droppeth as the gentle rain from heaven upon the place beneath. It is twice blest; it blesseth him that gives and him that takes."—*William Shakespeare*

SEE FOR YOURSELF

One of the original examples of righteousness is Abraham. Even before God gave Moses all the laws to write down and enforce, we are told that "Abra[ha]m believed the Lord, and the Lord declared him righteous because of his faith" (Genesis 15:6). Abraham had shortcomings just like the rest of us, yet his God-given stamp of righteousness carries into the New Testament as an example that we need not be circumcised nor conform to any other practice other than simple faith in order to receive God's forgiveness and salvation.

thing—to justify God's miraculous salvation. And all we can do to receive it is to open our hearts to Him. We're accustomed to having to accomplish certain tasks before we get good stuff. No paycheck until we put in a good week's work. No dessert until we clean our plates. No vacation days until we put in sufficient hours at work/school. But when it comes to salvation, there are no strings attached. Jesus urges people to place their faith in Him and become a family member.

The joy of salvation is compared to other big events in life: marriage (Ephesians 5:31-32), birth (John 3:3), adoption (Ephesians 1:5), and even coming back to life after being dead (Luke 15:32). And it is only by God's grace that this big event can ever take place.

Mercy

A parallel to grace is mercy. If grace is "undeserved favor," mercy is "undeserved reprieve from punishment." God's grace allows us to receive wonderful things we don't deserve. His mercy allows us to avoid terrible things we *do* deserve.

God is aware of every hateful look, lustful thought, jealous motive, and selfish action. Just imagine if all your friends knew your every doubt, every sarcastic remark, behind-the-back comment, and other less-than-honorable action. It wouldn't take long to become a bitter loner. But God, in His great mercy, is always willing to hear our confessions and forgive us of all the offensive things we do to Him every day.

Righteousness

Righteousness is another important biblical doctrine we need to be aware of. Essentially, it means rightness before God, and refers as much to legal status as to moment-to-moment behavior. (Just as people can become Christians and not *act* like Christians, God may declare us righteous even when our actions fail to conform to His standards.) Like salvation, we cannot achieve righteousness on our own (Romans 3:20). Yet as part of God's salvation of sinful people, He declares them righteous. And if we respond properly to His involvement in our lives, we begin to regularly improve our conduct to adhere to a higher level of righteousness.

Justification

Justification is a term used to describe the righteous status of a believer. Between the final second a person spends as an unbeliever and the first second that he or she places faith in Jesus, the person's behavior, attitudes, and such can't possibly change all that much. But what *does* change is his or her standing before God. Based on what Jesus has done on our behalf, God responds to sincere faith by declaring the person "justified," and it's an official legal ruling that stands. If the person dies the next second, he or she will be granted God's blessing and forgiveness, and enter His kingdom even without having had an opportunity to do anything to prove a change of heart (Romans 3:23-26; 4:4-5). The act of God's justification is final.

In addition to giving us an official legal "okay" before God, justification erases previous sins and returns us to God's favor. Some people like to define justification as "just as if I hadn't sinned." Others argue that such a definition is a bit too simplistic because the eventual freedom from the burden of sin comes only as a result of the highest possible price required to counteract the vast, ugly sin of humanity. We can rejoice in our new standing before God, but it doesn't mean much until we consider *how* it was achieved.

Sanctification

Sanctification is frequently paired with justification. In the Old Testament when something was *sanctified*, that meant it was devoted to God—"set apart" from common use. This could be true of people, places, things, and even special days. In New Testament usage, sanctification refers both to the act of God in "setting apart" believers for His service when He saves them and gives them the Holy Spirit, and the process believers undergo to become more like their perfect Lord. Romans 6–8 provides a good explanation of the concept of sanctification, and the word is used frequently throughout the New Testament. In fact, the word *saint* is from the same root as *sanctification*.

Holiness

Holiness is somewhat akin to sanctification but is more basic. Holiness is an attribute of God. Again, the meaning relates to being "set

QUESTIONS?

Don't you have to be somebody special to be classified as a "saint"?

Some denominations designate only a few spiritually tested and proven individuals to appear on their list of "official" saints. Yet the New Testament definition of *saint* includes *any* believer. (The newer translations have begun to change "saints" to "believers" in most places where the word is used.) When a person's faith in Jesus results in salvation, the person is set apart from the world—in God's eyes, at least. The person may not behave at all saintly for a long time, but he or she is added to the list of saints (believers) in God's kingdom.

Atonement is not a frequent topic of discussion for most Christians today, and we may tend to take it for granted. Yet the Day of Atonement (Yom Kippur) was the most solemn day in the life of Old Testament Israelites, as well as for many modern-day Jews. If we read Leviticus 16 to get a feel for the sacrifices and ceremony required, we might begin to take Jesus' atonement for us more seriously as well.

apart," and God in His love and perfection is so apart from the rest of the world that we cannot comprehend the extent of difference. Yet believers are called to imitate and approach God's holiness. As we mentally set ourselves apart from the sinful trappings of the world and learn to focus more on "the realities of heaven" (Colossians 3:1), we can achieve a greater degree of holiness. We are first designated as "set apart" from sin, and then, with God's grace, we attempt to live up to that designation. We will never get all the way there until we get to heaven, but that's no excuse for not trying. The command is clear: "But now you must be holy in everything you do, just as God—who chose you to be his children—is holy. For he himself has said, 'You must be holy because I am holy'" (1 Peter 1:15-16).

Atonement

Atonement is what makes our righteousness and justification possible. Some people point out that the word defines itself: at-one-ment. But the root of the original Hebrew word has more to do with "covering." Suppose after a fine (expensive) meal at a restaurant you discover to your horror that you've left all money and credit cards at home. Your dining companion might grin at your dilemma and pay for the meal with the simple comment, "Gotcha covered." On a much grander scale, we find ourselves standing before God unable to pay for our own sins and gain entrance to His kingdom. But the atonement of Jesus at the cross ensures that he has "covered" the admission price for us. This concept is crucial to Christianity. Jesus covers (atones for) our sins because that's the only possible way to satisfy God's criteria for righteousness.

Propitiation

Propitiation is a two-dollar word to denote "a provision for mercy." It can be closely connected to atonement. God cannot "look the other way" in regard to our sin. Jesus' atonement is a covering, not a cover-up. So in theological lingo, the blood of Jesus was the propitiation for our sins. Jesus' sacrificial death was a legitimate provision to allow a holy God to forgive sin and justify sinful people. The price was paid.

The King James Version used the word *propitiation* in a few

places, but you don't hear it much these days. The KJV translation of Romans 3:25, for example, tells us that, "God hath set forth [Jesus] *to be* a propitiation through faith in his blood, to declare his righteousness for the remission of sins that are past, through the forbearance of God." The New Living Translation puts it this way: "For God sent Jesus to take the punishment for our sins and to satisfy God's anger against us."

It's not that God needs to be placated with sacrifices to keep Him from being angry, as is the case with the worship of certain other "gods." Yet in order for God to remain just while still forgiving sin, there must be a provision made for Him to do so. That provision—propitiation—was the blood of Jesus.

Reader's Choice

All these things are benefits of Christianity that we might never really comprehend. If we are unaware of them when we find ourselves amid the ongoing tug-of-war between God and Satan, then Satan's offers might sound quite attractive. But when we start to recall the extent of what God has *already* done, the choice should be, pardon the expression, a no-brainer.

We might spend a month or so praying fervently for a much-desired raise and promotion. If it doesn't come through, we find ourselves disappointed with God. Even though Jesus has already died for us, providing atonement, propitiation, grace, mercy, salvation, eternal life, and all the rest, our spiritual shortsightedness allows us to feel that God has let us down. If we cave in and resort to devilish tactics to secure the raise and promotion for ourselves, it just might work. Yet to do so is to callously disregard the sacrifice and innumerable gifts God graciously offers.

The aspects of salvation are foundational truths, and the Bible has much to say about securing a proper foundation. Our lives get quite weighty at times. If we have a godly foundation, no amount of weight is too much. But if we choose any other alternative, even the second-best foundations will face storms sufficient to topple everything we've tried to build.

TRIVIA TIDBIT

The highfalutin term for the theological doctrine of salvation as effected by Jesus is *soteriology*. It's something you'll probably never need to know, but by reading this chapter you've entered this fascinating field of study. And to make the most of the opportunity, the next time someone asks "What's new?" you can respond, truthfully, "Well, I've been boning up on my soteriology lately. What's new with you?"

SAYS WHO?

"The knowledge of sin is the beginning of salvation."—*Epicurus*

A frequent metaphor for God in Scripture is a Rock (Deuteronomy 32:4; 2 Samuel 22:2-3; Psalm 92:15; Isaiah 26:4; etc.). And in one of the more well-known parables of Jesus, He makes it clear that the wise man builds his house on the rock (Matthew 7:24-27).

Scripture urges us to settle for no foundation other than God. Yet the choice remains ours. The battle is ongoing, and both sides are enlisting soldiers. We must decide for whom we fight. To do nothing is tantamount to choosing Satan. And regardless of any self-satisfying benefits for this second option, the ultimate price is eternity outside of God's presence in (as we saw in the last chapter) a hot, hot place.

Questions to Ponder and/or Discuss

1. Are you aware of any of the teachings about salvation other than the Christian doctrine (Islam, Buddhism, cult teachings, etc.)? How do each of these other beliefs stack up to Christianity?

2. Below is the list of things God provides for believers. Determine to what extent you've been aware of each one during the past week. Evaluate using a scale of 1 ("Not at all") to 10 ("Maximum awareness"):

Salvation	1	2	3	4	5	6	7	8	9	10
Grace	1	2	3	4	5	6	7	8	9	10
Mercy	1	2	3	4	5	6	7	8	9	10
Righteousness	1	2	3	4	5	6	7	8	9	10
Justification	1	2	3	4	5	6	7	8	9	10
Sanctification	1	2	3	4	5	6	7	8	9	10
Holiness	1	2	3	4	5	6	7	8	9	10
Atonement	1	2	3	4	5	6	7	8	9	10
Propitiation	1	2	3	4	5	6	7	8	9	10

3. What, if anything, would you like to add to the list?

4. The Bible compares salvation to a warrior's helmet (Ephesians 6:17). Can you think of any personal examples where you have felt the protection that salvation can provide in a Christian's life?

CHAPTER FIVE

"KING JAMES BIBLES ARE IN THE LAST AISLE ON THE LEFT."

From God's Mouth to Your Eyes
THE BIBLE

Let's review. We've said that Christians believe in God—one God in three Persons: Father, Son, and Holy Spirit. God is loving, merciful, forgiving, holy, and perfect in every way. God created a whole lot of angels, some of whom have rebelled against Him. Whatever God stands for, Satan and his angels oppose. When God created human beings, they had the opportunity to heed the advice and warning of God, yet they chose to do just the opposite at the behest of Satan. After Adam and Eve deliberately disobeyed, all human beings since have been born under that stain of sin. Yet God graciously invites us back into His kingdom if we place our faith in His Son, the only antidote for the sin problem. So far, so good?

This is an oversimplification, of course, but the process of salvation is remarkably easy as far as *we* are concerned. We place our faith in Jesus, God forgives us and seals us with His Holy Spirit, and it's a done deal. That part couldn't be simpler. It's when we attempt to understand all the spiritual concepts and complications of what God had to do in order to forgive us that the theology gets more complex.

SOME THINGS YOU'LL DISCOVER IN THIS CHAPTER

1. The uniqueness of the Bible in a world filled with books

2. Why the Bible is considered authoritative for Christian living

3. How a person's views about inspiration and inerrancy influence his or her opinion about the Bible

47

And just because you make a decision to become a Christian doesn't mean the devil is through with you. Far from it! If Satan doesn't prevent you from making that decision, the next best thing (from his perspective) is to impede your progress.

Since the battle going on all around us is spiritual and unseen, it's easy for us mere mortals to miss it. And if we just drift through life unaware of the spiritual issues at hand, Satan will take our apathy as a personal victory. Just because you decide to become a Christian doesn't mean you automatically become a spiritual warrior; it simply means you're wearing a different uniform. But if you don't get actively involved in the fray, your decision to become a Christian doesn't do the kingdom much good. A reluctant soldier is almost as good (or as bad) as no soldier at all.

Your God-given free will still comes into play. Even after making the decision to receive all the good stuff God has to offer (salvation, eternal life in heaven, etc.), you must choose to continue the process of spiritual growth and maturity. It is at this stage where essentially all Christians face periods of lethargy and/or defeat. It's just too easy to get involved with all the things we *can* see—homework, bosses, dirty laundry, messy kids, a graduate degree, or whatever. All the unseen powers around us continue to battle as we sit on the sidelines and argue about whether to have Chinese food or pizza tonight.

So what's a new Christian to do in order to keep his or her mind focused on God? Regardless of the impact of an initial salvation experience, if changes aren't made, time will take the fizz out of the bubbly feelings and quench the fires of spiritual passion that initially burned hot.

The people of faith in the Old Testament had a harder time of things. Even though it may seem that God was popping in to speak to them on a regular basis, years or decades between "personal" appearances were common. A dream here; an angelic visit there; a burning bush on one occasion. In a couple extreme cases, a talking donkey and a manifestation within a fiery furnace. But usually the person was left in the wake of an enormous job assignment with a tiny bit of comprehension and a large amount of faith.

These days believers have it much better. While we may not see or hear God as Moses and Abraham did, most of us have access to His Word on a regular basis. So let's see what Christians believe about the Bible.

Every Day I Read the Book

No matter what people think about the accuracy and inspiration of the Bible, most will readily admit it is a book unlike any other. It was written over a period of 1,400 years or so (from the time of Moses to the end of the first century) by around 40 different "authors" using a great diversity of writing styles (narrative, poetry, prophecy, parable, apocalyptic literature, etc.). And yet it maintains an astounding consistency in theme cohesion. It is truly a marvel of a work.

Where people tend to disagree about the significance of the Bible is in its source, its inspiration, its trustworthiness, and its usefulness to people today. So let's examine some of these key points.

The Inspiration of the Bible

To begin with, most Christians believe the Bible is not just a collection of *good* words, but literally *God's* Word. We might read and benefit from the collected wisdom of Confucius, Shakespeare, or any other number of classic writers. But if we believe God is the source of everything written in Scripture, we must give the Bible much more credence than anything else we read.

In one of Paul's letters to Timothy, he made it clear that all Scripture is "inspired by God," or to use another interpretation, "All Scripture is God-breathed" (2 Timothy 3:16, NIV). Tradition says that Moses wrote the first five books of the Bible, getting some special insight from God about creation and witnessing other remarkable things about God first-hand. The prophets recorded some wonderful miracles of God, as well as some horrendous things taking place in their culture at the time. Matthew, Mark, Luke, and John each wrote a biography of Jesus. Luke added a book of church history (Acts). Paul, Peter, James, and others wrote letters. John saw a phenomenal vision and recorded it (Revelation).

Behind the pens of each of these authors was the inspiration of the

SAYS WHO?

"Had the Bible been in clear straightforward language, had the ambiguities and contradictions been edited out, and had the language been constantly modernized to accord with contemporary taste it would almost certainly have been, or become, a work of lesser influence."
—*John Kenneth Galbraith*

SEE FOR YOURSELF

"All Scripture is inspired by God and is useful to teach us what is true and to make us realize what is wrong in our lives. It straightens us out and teaches us to do what is right. It is God's way of preparing us in every way, fully equipped for every good thing God wants us to do." (2 Timothy 3:16-17)

QUESTIONS?

Why do some Bibles have the Apocrypha and others don't? How did people decide what writings should become official Scripture while others shouldn't?

As you might expect, with all the "religious" writings over the centuries, when it came time to collect the official sacred writings in one book, there was considerable discussion about what to leave in and what to leave out—but not as much disagreement as you might expect. Later chapters will explain why the Roman Catholic Church kept the books of the Apocrypha while others rejected them. We will also see how stringent were the councils that made the decisions, as well as how the "canon" (standard) of Scripture was determined.

Spirit of God. The humans wrote what they saw and felt, but God was orchestrating it all. They weren't ghostwriters; they were Holy Ghost writers. Peter made this point very clear: "Above all, you must understand that no prophecy in Scripture ever came from the prophets themselves or because they wanted to prophesy. It was the Holy Spirit who moved the prophets to speak from God" (2 Peter 1:20-21).

So it logically follows that if we believe God is behind everything in the Bible—that Scripture is literally His Word—then we are compelled to treat it differently than any other work of literature on our shelves. You might read a Peter Drucker book about how to operate a business, a Martha Stewart tome on home décor, an Emeril book about preparing a Cajun feast, or Stephen Hawking's description of the origins of time and space. These people are each experts in their fields with much to offer, yet you would have the liberty of disagreeing, forming your own opinions, or skipping any parts that didn't particularly interest you. That's because regardless of how highly any author might think of himself or herself, nobody's manuscript starts out as "God-breathed."

But since most Christians believe that *all* Scripture is inspired by God, it is important that we don't skip over big sections or come up with a "better" way to do things. God reveals Himself to us in the Bible, and we need to formulate as complete a picture as possible. Suppose your spouse or someone very close wrote you a five-page letter explaining, "This will tell you my deepest thoughts and feelings." How do you think he or she would feel if your reply the next week was, "I only read the third paragraph of page four, but it was pretty good"?

The better we understand the totality of the Scriptures, the better we will understand what God is trying to tell us about Himself—and about us! This is why many Christians are so insistent on Bible reading. It's not just a good thing to do; it's a primary way that God communicates with us. It is inspired and inspiring.

The Inerrancy of the Bible

Of course, it is difficult to get excited about something if we don't trust it. Therefore, most Christians believe that the Bible is not only inspired by God, but also is without error.

However, not everyone can endorse the concept of the Bible being infallible and inerrant. Some such people have no argument with what we've said so far about inspiration. Certainly the God-breathed information begins without error. But where sinful people are involved, they say, mistakes are bound to be made. Maybe someone didn't hear God right. Maybe he wrote it down wrong. Maybe over the years, the truths of Scripture have become muddled like the message of a circle of people playing the gossip parlor game.

Yet the proponents of biblical inerrancy hold that when the Holy Spirit is involved in something, it is done correctly. There is no doubt that the human authors of Scripture were sinful just as the rest of us are. But the Holy Spirit endowed them with special gifts, and they performed to the highest levels of truth and accuracy—in regard to their writings, at least. Therefore, everything in the Bible can be trusted.

Deep within our hearts we might tend to question the reliability of some of the mysteries of the Bible—creation, Noah and the ark, Jonah in the belly of the great fish, Lot's wife turning to a pillar of salt, and other things. But we desperately want to believe Jesus and everything He has done to provide salvation. And in the wonderful complexities of biblical truth, Jesus made a reference to each of these stories—verifying them for new generations of believers. If we believe in Jesus, we can take confidence that He assures us of the truth of every "smallest detail" of the Old Testament (Matthew 5:17-18).

In debates with the religious elite of His time, Jesus used what most of us would consider obscure portions of the Old Testament. In doing so, He demonstrated that all of Scripture is not only inspired by God but is without error.

TRIVIA TIDBIT

Emperor Menelik II, the African ruler credited with establishing Ethiopia, did more than *read* his Bible for help. When ill, he would literally eat a few pages to restore his health. But after suffering a stroke, he ate the entire book of Kings and died of a bowel obstruction. (Don't try this at home.)

Look into My I's

We tend to use a lot of words interchangeably when it comes to describing the Bible. But below are some key words with more precise definitions:

QUESTIONS?

Doesn't it stand to reason that with all the copying and translating done throughout the centuries the Bible may have picked up a few mistakes here and there?

A tremendous amount of care went into seeing that detail and accuracy were maintained while hand-copying Scriptures. And while a few manuscripts contain what appears to be a scribal inaccuracy or two, nothing of serious consequence is called into question. That's one reason the discovery of the Dead Sea Scrolls was such a big deal. They confirmed the accuracy of other existing manuscripts beyond a doubt. Based on documented evidence, it's more logical to doubt the authenticity and accuracy of Shakespeare, Homer, or many other early writers than those who wrote what became sacred Scripture.

SAYS WHO?

"If there be any mistakes in the Bible there may well be a thousand. If there is one falsehood in that Book it did not come from the God of truth."
—*John Wesley*

- *Inspiration*—The work of the Holy Spirit in guiding the personalities and talents of human authors to enable them to record God's Word with divine authority and without error.
- *Illumination*—The work of the Holy Spirit in helping believers comprehend the truth of the Bible.
- *Inerrancy*—The belief that the Bible is without error.
- *Infallibility*—Being incapable of error, especially in regard to matters of faith or morals.

As with most topics of Christianity and theology, you will find various levels of agreement when it comes to the inspiration, inerrancy, and the other "I's" related to Scripture. Fine lines may be drawn with regard to some of these definitions and beliefs.

For example, it is possible to believe (because some people do) that the Bible is not inerrant, yet is infallible. In other words, it might have a glitch or two, but never where it comes to essential eternal matters. Some people believe that *portions* of the Bible are definitely inspired, while others aren't. They contend that some parts of the Bible could have been written just as well by an expert in history as by someone inspired by God. Others suggest that the inspiration of Scripture has more to do with the underlying *concepts* than the exact wording.

But whenever the inerrancy of Scripture is questioned, the obvious dilemma is, "How can we be confident about *anything* once we make allowance for error?" If you can't bring yourself to believe the Creation account as presented in Scripture, for example, can you really put your faith in the doctrinal teaching that God makes us "new persons" when we become Christians (2 Corinthians 5:17)? If the Noah account is thought to be more fable than fact, can we really trust God the next time our own crises come flooding down on us?

Another consideration is that God is much smarter than we are, and He doesn't expect us to know everything He does. So when Jesus makes reference to the mustard seed as being "the smallest of all seeds" (Matthew 13:32), does that mean the Bible is in error when scientists discover orchid seeds that are even smaller? Didn't Jesus know about those other, even tinier seeds?

Of course He did! But in making a point contrasting small seeds with large plants, He limited His teaching to the awareness of His listeners. For all they knew, mustard seeds were the smallest seeds around. To introduce teachings about orchids, which weren't exactly plentiful in the Sinai desert, would have been unnecessarily confusing and complex.

We need to remember that the Bible is primarily a book to help us comprehend spiritual truth. Attempting to use its first-century writings as a 21st-century science or social studies textbook may not be a good idea, but that in no way dims the light of truth it shines upon spiritual matters.

So although not all Christians believe in the complete inspiration and inerrancy of Scripture, many do. If God made a personal appearance every time He wanted to tell us something, most Christians would be filled with fear, if not beset by heart attacks. Therefore, it's helpful to begin by consulting what God has *already* said in His Word.

Scripture is a rule book for what to do and what not to do. It's a call to action; it provides clear marching orders as we seek direction in life. It provides access to God's will and acts as a light to illuminate which paths to take in many of the unclear portions of our lives. And as we seek to relate to God in deeper ways, it provides us with numerous eyewitness accounts of Jesus' life—a perfect model of what God expects of us and how He wants to interact with us.

Christians seeking God's will for their lives but not frequently consulting the Bible are likely to be frustrated. But those who begin with regular Bible reading, study, and meditation are certain to make numerous discoveries that will enlighten them and point them in specific directions. If we desire for God to speak clearly to us, perhaps we first should see what He has *already* said. Many times, that's all we need to know.

And sometimes God speaks to us through other people. That's a consideration we will deal with in the next chapter.

TRIVIA TIDBIT

The theory and methodology of interpreting of scriptural texts is known as *hermeneutics.*

SEE FOR YOURSELF

Below are some images biblical writers use to describe God's Word.
- A lamp for my feet and a light for my path (Psalm 119:105)
- Fire (Jeremiah 23:29)
- A hammer that smashes rock to pieces (Jeremiah 23:29)
- Seed that needs proper nourishment to grow (Mark 4:1-20)
- The sword of the Spirit (Ephesians 6:17)
- A mirror that reflects changes that need to be made (James 1:22-25)

Questions to Ponder and/or Discuss

1. Consider the following portions of the Bible. In each case, determine first whether or not you've read that part. Then determine whether or not you understand it to your satisfaction.

	READ THIS?	UNDERSTAND IT?
Old Testament law	☐	☐
Old Testament narrative (the basic stories)	☐	☐
The era of the judges	☐	☐
The reigns of Saul/David/Solomon	☐	☐
Other kings of Israel/Judah	☐	☐
The writings (Psalms, Proverbs, etc.)	☐	☐
The major prophets	☐	☐
The minor prophets	☐	☐
The life of Jesus	☐	☐
The teachings/parables of Jesus	☐	☐
Church history (book of Acts)	☐	☐
Paul's letters	☐	☐
Other writers' letters	☐	☐
book of Revelation	☐	☐

2. What are your personal opinions regarding the inspiration and inerrancy of Scripture? (Be honest about any doubts and concerns you may have.)

3. Review the following biblical images used to describe God's Word. Can you apply one or more of them to your personal Bible-reading experience?

A lamp for my feet and a light for my path
Fire
A hammer that smashes rock to pieces
Seeds that need proper nourishment to grow
The sword of the Spirit
A mirror that reflects changes that need to be made

"GREAT SERMON, PASTOR! I ESPECIALLY LIKE THE PART ABOUT THE SOWER AND THE SEED."

Get Thee to a Church
DOCTRINAL ASPECTS OF THE CHURCH

SOME THINGS YOU'LL DISCOVER IN THIS CHAPTER

1. The mission of the Christian church

2. The primary position of Jesus in connection with the church

3. Variations in week-to-week church operation

While the Bible is usually the best place to begin when establishing and maintaining a proper relationship with God, it's not all Christians have going for them. Sometimes it's a tempting proposition to grab a Bible, climb a hill, and begin to interact with God. Indeed, we speak of "mountaintop experiences," where we feel that God is very close to us. Yet if that's *all* we're doing, and if we aren't careful, there is a tendency to begin to feel above the rest of the Christian world as well. If we discover we're looking down on others, we've lost the proper perspective.

Becoming a Christian must be an individual decision. No one else can do it for you. You have the free will to make a decision to believe in God or not, and no one else can exert veto power to "pray you into heaven" without your consent.

Yet even though becoming a Christian is an individual choice, Christianity is by no means intended to be a solo journey. Your spiritual growth and progress will continue to be your individual

SAYS WHO?

"The church is not a gallery for the exhibition of eminent Christians, but a school for the education of imperfect ones."
—*Henry Ward Beecher*

QUESTIONS?

What if I'm trying to get along with my fellow churchgoers, but another person and I have had an argument and just can't seem to come to terms? Won't the church be affected if we both continue to attend?

Yes, conflict between any two people within the church is likely to affect the entire church. That's why in such cases the church has a biblical mandate to be the "court of last resort" for the conflict. If you can't settle it one-on-one, or even two- or three-on-one, then the church should address the problem and bring it to an end. (See Matthew 18:15-20.) So rather than one or both of you avoiding church, it's yet another reason to attend!

responsibility, yet you must also learn to work and play well with all the other Christians who have made the same decision. Christianity requires a certain amount of structure to meet people's needs, teach and train new believers, and continue to spread the good news about Jesus. That's where the church comes in.

We will take a *historic* look at the first-century church in Chapter 8. But in this chapter we want to take more of a doctrinal approach about what Christians believe in regard to the *contemporary* church.

Church Chat

The word *church* can mean a number of different things. We speak of a new church going up on the corner, referring to a building. We speak of "going to church," meaning a group which gathers at a certain location. We speak of the church of Jesus Christ, meaning the collective body of people, living and dead, who have professed faith in Jesus as Lord and Savior. Some have even been known to ask, "So, do you want to do church this week?" which tends to relegate "church" to a social activity akin to racquetball or eating out. Yet each of these references suggests that "church" involves more than merely a relationship between the individual and God.

Therefore, we must learn to interact properly with other Christians as well as with God—a task that is frequently harder than it sounds. As we will see in future chapters, the reason so many different denominations exist today is because one group of Christians couldn't see eye to eye with another group of Christians, and as a result the two groups went their separate ways. Eventually one or both of those groups took sides and split again, and so on and so forth.

Yet in spite of the doctrinal nitpicking that has taken place over the centuries, most Christian groups have a number of foundational beliefs they *do* agree on. Primary among these beliefs is the conviction that Jesus is key to anything else that happens in the church.

Jesus is the church's cornerstone

If you think of God's "church" in terms of a building, with each believer representing a different "stone" or "brick" in the big picture, then Jesus is the cornerstone (Matthew 21:42-44; Ephesians 2:20-21). This symbol indicates He is first and foremost among the other pieces (Colossians 1:18). He is the primary piece of the church. Without it, the building would not stand, at least, not for long.

Jesus is the foundation of the church

But even more basic to a building than the cornerstone is its foundation, and other places in Scripture use this imagery to describe Jesus' place in the church. At the end of the Sermon on the Mount is Jesus' reminder that, "Anyone who listens to my teaching and obeys me is wise, like a person who builds a house on solid rock" (Matthew 7:24). Any less solid foundation will crumble whenever storms hit. Later Paul challenges his readers to be careful as they build on the foundation Jesus has provided for them.

If the church is to be strong and vital in the world, Christians must acknowledge Jesus as the foundation and begin to build on that foundation with actions that will have lasting value. As many people know well, it's not hard to be a regular church attendee without actually getting involved in what's going on. But such noncommittal actions are the equivalent of spiritual Tinkertoys for supposedly mature Christians. Such "wooden" actions may not count for much when tested by fire.

Jesus is the head of the church

So far it may sound as if you need to be an architect to comprehend the nature of the church. All this talk about foundations and cornerstones may seem a bit impersonal. But the church is also symbolized as a *person.*

In fact, this symbol has become so common that we may frequently refer to our local church *body.* The imagery used in Scripture is that each believer has specific spiritual gifts, allowing him or her to serve as a "part" of the body—eye, ear, hand, foot, or whatever (1 Corinthians 12:12-21). But Jesus is the "head" of the body (Colossians 1:18).

It's comforting to know that we don't have to depend on ourselves or one of our peers to be the "brains" of this operation—that's all up to Jesus. But just as the various parts of a properly function-

TRIVIA TIDBIT

In ancient civilizations, the laying of the foundation stone of a building was sometimes accompanied by human sacrifice. Archaeologists have unearthed numerous skeletons along with cornerstones. It is not even uncommon to find the skeletons of infants buried in clay jars. As horrendous as the custom was, it might remind us that Jesus' honored role of cornerstone was not accomplished without a gruesome sacrifice of His own.

SEE FOR YOURSELF

"For no one can lay any other foundation than the one we already have—Jesus Christ. Now anyone who builds on that foundation may use gold, silver, jewels, wood, hay, or straw. But there is going to come a time of testing at the judgment day to see what kind of work each builder has done. Everyone's work will be put through the fire to see whether or not it keeps its value" (1 Corinthians 3:11-13).

SEE FOR YOURSELF

"Think of ways to encourage one another to outbursts of love and good deeds. And let us not neglect our meeting together, as some people do, but encourage and warn each other, especially now that the day of [Jesus'] coming back again is drawing near" (Hebrews 10:24-25).

ing body receive signals from the brain in order to work together, so the members of a church should respond to Jesus' direction for how they live and act. Otherwise, the church body is likely to need life support just to keep breathing, much less walk around and accomplish anything.

Jesus is the husband of the church

In perhaps the most intimate analogy of how Jesus and the church should interact, we are given the image of a marriage—husband and wife (2 Corinthians 11:2). Many people recall their wedding day as one of the most special days (if not *the* most special) in their lives. And just as one's spouse is the reason to celebrate a wedding, each believer's relationship with Jesus is basic to the success of any church gathering.

At first it might not be apparent what a cornerstone, a building's foundation, a human body, and a groom have in common. But in these images of how Jesus relates to the church, we see the recurring theme of unity and cooperation. No matter how strong the church seems to be, without Jesus it is like a building without a cornerstone or foundation, a headless body, or a widowed bride.

From a Church to a Mission

So now we know where the church stands. It stands on the firm foundation of Jesus Christ, built upon an unshakable cornerstone. It stands as a bride at the altar, uniting forever with a beloved groom. And it stands as a body in response to its head, stronger and more assured as the individual parts better learn to work with one another.

But now what? Are *we* just supposed to stand around as well?

The overall mission of the church is pretty clear. As a body of believers, we have been charged to do a number of things. Let's take a look at some of them.

Worship together

As we have seen, both the Old Testament and New Testament models show the importance of not just serving God as solitary "Christian soldiers" but also coming together regularly to see how the rest of the troops are doing and to unite in worship of God. The overall concept of worship is to acknowledge God's position as sovereign in the universe. While individual churches may vary on what they emphasize, the biblical model for corporate worship includes preaching, reading Scripture, prayer, music/singing, giving, and perhaps a few other things.

Another element of worship is participation in the sacraments (or ordinances). As we will see later, churches vary as to the number of sacraments that should be practiced and the methods used to administer them. Yet two are almost universal among all churches: the Lord's Supper (or Eucharist) and baptism.

Baptism is not exclusively a Christian rite, though it usually serves as a public demonstration of one's identification with a particular group. Christians are baptized to show their inclusion in the body of believers and/or a local congregation. In addition, many see baptism as an external demonstration of an inner change—the symbolic death of the old, sinful person and the coming to life of a new believer. Other churches baptize infants in anticipation of their coming to faith at a later time.

The specific method of baptism varies as well, with sprinkling, pouring, and full immersion being the primary options. A case can be made for each of these methods, and some churches are quite firm about which one is appropriate and which two aren't. Other churches note that *all* the options are symbolic and don't place undue emphasis on any single method of baptism.

The Lord's Supper was instituted by Jesus at His last supper when He passed around bread and wine, stating that the bread was His body and the wine His blood. Essentially all churches feel this is an important ordinance to be continued until Jesus returns, yet again they don't agree as to specifics. To many churches, the bread and wine (or juice) are *symbols* of Jesus' broken body and shed blood. Other churches, however, believe that the Eucharist is one of the mysteries of God. Although we can't fully understand the hows and whys, they believe the bread and wine literally become the body and blood of Jesus in sacramental form, although no change takes

SAYS WHO?

"What a vast distance there is between knowing God and loving Him!"
—*Blaise Pascal*

61

place in appearance, taste, or texture. Somehow the Holy Spirit changes the bread and wine into the substance of the body and blood of Jesus Christ.

Common to all the options is that the sacraments should shift our focus from ourselves to God. The Lord's Supper reminds us that the reason we assemble as a church is because Jesus suffered and died to achieve our forgiveness and salvation. And baptism indicates that we willingly leave behind our old ways in order to be "reborn" as one of His children.

Uphold the Great Commission

In what were perhaps Jesus' final words to His followers, He spoke what has come to be known as the Great Commission (Matthew 28:18-20). In a few sentences, He instructed His listeners to make new disciples, baptize them, and teach them to obey the commands He had provided. These actions are certainly key to the mission and purpose of any church today.

Delve into the mysteries of God

Some of what Christians believe is mysterious and perplexing (which is perhaps why you bought this book). As individuals we struggle with certain portions of Scripture as we try to remain open to the Holy Spirit's wisdom and insight. And while we do, the church is a powerful resource to help us explore these deeper truths (1 Corinthians 4:1). God may use your pastor, a guest speaker, a Sunday school teacher, or an unlikely member of your small group to illumine your thinking in an unexpected way. It's part of the design of each person using his or her gifts for the benefit of the entire body.

Reconcile people to God

Sometimes you might visit a church that is doing much of what we say its mission *should* be, yet it seems to be somewhat off target. It's easy to fall into patterns and do things mechanically rather than always operating from a genuine heartfelt passion for ministry. Paul reminds us that one crucial reason the church preaches, makes disciples, gives to the poor, and all the other things is the importance of reconciling people to God (2 Corinthians 5:18-19).

Churches, Churches, Churches: So Many Options

For two millennia now, these have been some basic goals of Christian churches worldwide. This week if you attend a Christian church in your neighborhood, you're likely to encounter these same things in one form or another. But it's that "one form or another" that gets very disconcerting for some people.

As you visit a variety of Christian churches, the vast array of church formats you find can be confusing. When we go beyond *what* the basic mission of the church is and into *how* a church should operate, we soon run into a lot of debate and disagreement. Consider just a few basics:

- Who is primarily responsible for this particular church? (The pastor? The denomination? A board or council?)
- How should the leadership of the church be structured? (Just a pastor/priest? An official staff? A combination of paid staff and laypeople?)
- What do you call the leaders? (Deacons? Elders? Presbyters? Bishops?)
- Who has final authority? (The congregation? The denomination? The nation?)
- Can women be involved in leadership? (Fully? Partially? Not at all?)
- What sacraments are included in the regular worship services? (Baptism? The Lord's Supper? Confirmation? Confession? Foot washing?)
- What is included in a normal worship service? What ministries, if any, are pursued outside the local church? (Missions? Charitable work?)

We are hard-pressed to label most of the variations of church tradition "right" or "wrong." Each denomination and individual church attempts to determine what is best, and still the results run the gamut from very formal to freewheeling, from quiet and hushed to bold and boisterous. (Again, later chapters will explore the basic reasons for much of this difference of opinion.)

TRIVIA TIDBIT

The *2001 New York Times Almanac* reports the following statistics for Christian churches in the United States:
Number of local congregations 349,506
Total clergy 534,913
Total membership 158,294,022

Ninety percent of church members belong to one of the 30 top denominations. There are, of course, numerous other denominations (as well as divisions within the top 30). The Roman Catholic Church claims just over 39 percent of the total members. The largest Protestant group is the Southern Baptist Convention, with just under 10 percent.

QUESTIONS?

With all the choices of churches, how do I pick one that's right for me?

If you have denominational ties, you might want to start there simply because you'll have some idea of what to expect. Then talk to friends and find out where they go and what they like/dislike about their own churches. And since nothing beats firsthand experience, visit a number of churches and see where God seems more active. As you visit, ask about each church's basic beliefs. Most places will be more than happy to give you a printed doctrinal statement.

Some people point to the imperfections of the churches they visit as excuses to avoid regular attendance. Or they cite a particular belief or custom and decide they simply can't tolerate it and therefore don't get involved in a church at all. And since no church is perfect, such people will never find one that can meet their impossible standards.

However, it's only a matter of time until all believers—the entire church—are going to be united. The Bible teaches that in eternity, the church is still active in its primary mission: to worship God. At that time the outreach will have come to an end. People will be reconciled to God, or they won't. The mysteries will all be explained. But the worship will continue forever. John's vision in Revelation repeatedly emphasizes the intensity of this heavenly worship (4:1-11; 5:11-14; 7:9-17; 11:16-18; etc.).

The church here and now is going to become the church in eternity, so playing hooky or making excuses is only delaying the inevitable. All believers who are physically able ought to be involved on a regular basis. Indeed, one reason we need to devote ourselves to a local church, as well as to God, is because we are supposed to become more and more like Jesus as we prepare for eternity with Him (1 John 3:1-3). Regular attendance at a church not only allows us to benefit from the spiritual gifts of others, but allows them to benefit from *our* gifts as well.

As we have said, we'll take another look at the church in Chapters 8–11, next time from a historical perspective. In the meantime, give some additional thought to the importance of church at a doctrinal level. Just as the Bible provides God's guidance and insight on a personal level, the church serves as His way of reaching us through other people.

We'll leave you with a list of reasons why regular attendance in a local church can be beneficial for you. If you're still not quite persuaded by the personal satisfaction and peace that God provides to His obedient followers, the next chapter provides yet another good reason that we need to remain faithful and active in the work of God.

Ten Reasons to Be Committed to a Local Church

1. Because minimum regular attendance requires approximately one of your 168 hours each week. Shouldn't we devote as much time to God and others as we spend stuck in traffic or waiting to log onto the Internet?

2. Because life is sprinkled, if not filled, with pain and tragedy (Ecclesiastes 9:12). Regular church involvement provides the antidote of hope and faith, and reminds us we need not suffer alone.

3. Because many worthwhile pursuits in life require discipline before they're beneficial and/or enjoyable (losing weight, working out, learning to play an instrument, etc.). The same is true of church. First you discipline yourself to attend, and later you discover the enjoyment and satisfaction (1 Corinthians 9:24-27).

4. Because all the "religious stuff" that sounds so confusing at first begins to make sense over time (1 Corinthians 1:18-31).

5. Because you can learn a lot from older and/or more experienced Christians (Titus 2:3-8), and because you have a lot to offer the rest of the church body, which you may not even know about until you are regularly involved (1 Corinthians 12:4-7).

6. Because you cease to be the center of the universe, so your own problems and complaints start looking smaller (1 Peter 5:6-9).

7. Because regular interaction with the real God reveals the insufficiency of all the other "idols" we tend to depend on (Habakkuk 2:18-20).

8. Because like a soldier in a war, you get much closer to other people when you're attempting to resist a common enemy (James 4:7-12).

9. Because church involves believers in sacraments and/or traditions of faith that are inspirational and uplifting (1 Corinthians 11:23-26; 12:13).

10. Because God says we should attend (Hebrews 10:25).

Once you discover what church involvement can do for you, you'll never again be happy without it. But don't take our word for it. See for yourself!

Questions to Ponder and/or Discuss

1. Which of the following best expresses your opinions about church?

   _ Bunch of hypocrites, if you ask me.

   _ Nice enough group of people, but just not my thing.

   _ I don't know enough about it to have formed an opinion.

   _ I enjoy it the two times I go each year.

   _ I'm so involved it's more routine than meaningful to me these days.

   _ Love it. Wouldn't drop out for anything.

   _ Other:

2. If you're regularly involved in a church, how much do you know about its doctrinal statement? The denomination? The structure and government?

3. Think of the last church service you attended and give a grade to each of the following things:

   Group worship of God

   Upholding the Great Commission (Making disciples, teaching, baptizing, etc.)

   Better understanding the mysteries of God

   Reconciling people to God

CHAPTER SEVEN

Doomsday's Rockin' Eve Countdown

THE END TIMES

Expectation is motivation. If students never expected a quiz, many would never study the material with any intensity. When employees stop anticipating the possibility of raises and/or promotions, their productivity tends to level off, if not nose-dive. When we're expecting company, we tend to care a bit more than usual about how the house looks and how recently the toilet has been scrubbed.

The expected event might be positive (a visit from a loved one) or negative (a subpoena to appear in court). Either way, the anticipation of the event tends to motivate us to action in order to be better prepared.

And so it is with Christians. One of the basic underlying doctrines of the church is that Jesus will someday return, judge the wicked, reward the righteous, and establish His eternal kingdom. If Christians really believe this is going to happen, and perhaps happen soon, they will behave one way. If they don't believe this or haven't given the possibility adequate thought, they are less likely to be motivated to be on guard at all times.

And while Christians have varying beliefs about most of the

SOME THINGS YOU'LL DISCOVER IN THIS CHAPTER

1. Some of the things we can expect during the end times

2. Various viewpoints about the end times schedule.

3. What we can be sure of amid all the confusing signs and symbols

SAYS WHO?

"The doctrine of the Second Coming teaches us that we do not and cannot know when the world drama will end. The curtain may be rung down at any moment: say, before you have finished reading this paragraph."—*C. S. Lewis*

specifics of their faith, the confusion is perhaps never more intense than when it comes to what's going to happen during the end times. Even those who agree that certain events are scheduled to take place frequently debate the *order* of those events. It will be our goal in this chapter to list several of the expected events and provide a few outlooks that attempt to organize and make sense of those events.

Misfortune Telling

The following elements are all included in discussions about the end times. We'll first look at a number of people and events we're told to expect, and then we'll try them in a number of different orders to see which, if any, make sense.

The Great Tribulation

The prophet Daniel wrote of a visit from the angel Gabriel who foretold a time of unprecedented war and rebellion. Among other things, he tells us:

> A period of seventy sets of seven has been decreed for your people and your holy city to put down rebellion, to bring an end to sin, to atone for guilt, to bring in everlasting righteousness, to confirm the prophetic vision, and to anoint the Most Holy Place. Now listen and understand! Seven sets of seven plus sixty-two sets of seven will pass from the time the command is given to rebuild Jerusalem until the Anointed One comes. Jerusalem will be rebuilt with streets and strong defenses, despite the perilous times.
>
> After this period of sixty-two sets of seven, the Anointed One will be killed, appearing to have accomplished nothing, and a ruler will arise whose armies will destroy the city and the temple. The end will come with a flood, and war and its miseries are decreed from that time to the very end. He will make a treaty with the people for a period of one set of seven, but after half this time, he will put an end to the

sacrifices and offerings. Then as a climax to all his terrible deeds, he will set up a sacrilegious object that causes desecration, until the end that has been decreed is poured out on this defiler. (Daniel 9:24-27)

This can be confusing prophecy, and it is interpreted in various ways, yet it should not be overlooked. Jesus later made a reference to this prophecy and added that what Daniel was describing would be "a time of greater horror than anything the world has ever seen or will ever see again" (Matthew 24:15-22). The phrase "great tribulation" was designated by John in the book of Revelation (7:14).

Some people feel the great tribulation includes all the bad stuff that has happened to Christians throughout the centuries since Jesus lived. It has been said that more Christians died for their faith in the 20th century than in all the previous centuries combined. However, other people feel that "the great tribulation" refers to a specific, designated time still in the future.

TRIVIA TIDBIT

A "judgment seat" was an elevated bench where a judge would hear arguments. Jesus appeared at such a place during His trial, submitting to the judgment of others just prior to His crucifixion (Matthew 27:19; John 19:13). But now Jesus is the judge, and at some point in the future we're all scheduled to stand before *His* judgment seat to hear His verdict for us (Romans 14:10; 2 Corinthians 5:10).

The Judgments of God

The book of Revelation goes into considerable detail in describing a sequence of events that God will inflict upon a world filled with rebellious and wicked people. This is where we find the biblical reference to what have become known as the four horsemen of the Apocalypse (Revelation 6:1-8). But that's just the beginning of the terrible things yet to come. The apostle John describes Jesus popping seals on a scroll, each of which unleashes nasty stuff upon the earth. Later a series of angels sound trumpets (Revelation 8–11) and another group pour out "bowls of God's wrath" (Revelation 16), each of which triggers a horribly destructive event. The repeated emphasis is that these plagues and sufferings are God's judgments on evil people who simply refuse to repent.

Armageddon

One of the "bowl judgments" triggers international hostility that will escalate into the bloodiest war of all time. It will also be the final war in earth's history. Located near the mountain and city named Meggido, the identification of Armageddon (Revelation

QUESTIONS?

When the Bible speaks of "the Day of the Lord," is it a reference to Jesus' second coming?

The "day" is not necessarily a 24-hour period. It refers to a spiritual turning of the tide that will include God's final victory over His enemies, Jesus' second coming, final judgment, and the abolishment of sin. Finally, the Day of the Lord will also usher in a new heaven and new earth where God and His people are completely reconciled. (See Matthew 24; Luke 21:7-33; 1 Thessalonians 5:2-3; 2 Thessalonians 2:1-3; and Revelation 21:1.)

16:16) is assumed by some to be a specific geographic location. Others feel it is more of a general reference not confined to a particular place. Armageddon is mentioned only once in Scripture, yet has become well-known as a place of finality and doom.

The Second Coming of Jesus

The New Testament refers to the return of Jesus more than 300 times. Jesus promised that He would return (John 14:3), and angels confirmed the fact (Acts 1:11). The Second Coming is foundational to several key teachings, as well as the subject of a number of Jesus' parables. Believers are regularly reminded of this coming event to encourage them to maintain hope and perseverance throughout hard times.

The Millennium

After all the Y2K hubbub, most people today are aware that *millennium* means "1,000 years." From a biblical perspective, *the* Millennium refers to an event mentioned in Revelation (20:1-15). In the apostle John's description, it is a time during which Satan will be bound and a specific group of martyrs will come back to life and reign with Jesus. Some Christians believe that Jesus will establish a kingdom on earth during this time.

The Rapture

The word "rapture" isn't found in Scripture. The term derives from the Latin word for "caught up," *rapturo*, which was used in the Latin translation of 1 Thessalonians 4:17: "Then, together with them, we who are still alive and remain on the earth will be caught up in the clouds to meet the Lord in the air and remain with him forever."

So the "rapture" refers to the "snatching up" of believers—an express passage from earth directly to heaven without the usual annoying necessity of dying. This event follows a resurrection of Christians who have died (1 Thessalonians 4:16), thereby uniting all believers in heaven.

The popular Left Behind series of books begins with the Rapture and then speculates about what might take place during the end times. Jesus also made what many interpret to be a reference to this event. In telling His disciples what to expect in regard to His return, He spoke of a time when "two people will be asleep in one bed; one will be taken away, and the other will be left. Two women will be grinding flour together at the mill; one will be taken, the other left" (Luke 17:34-35). In other words, the Rapture will be sudden and unexpected.

The Antichrist

While the world in general will oppose God in the last days, the head of the resistance is someone who has come to be referred to as the Antichrist. (The more common reference to him in Revelation is "the beast.") In one sense, anyone who stands against the work, teachings, and ministry of Jesus is considered an "antichrist" by this definition (1 John 2:18). However, many people expect this end-times personality to be a powerful, Satan-inspired figure who rallies people to oppose Jesus and the few who live for Him. At one point, anyone who refuses to pledge loyalty to the Antichrist and receive his mark on his or her body will be denied the right to buy or sell anything.

The Antichrist will have an equally devious sidekick, commonly referred to as the "false prophet." The two will work in tandem to deceive and destroy everyone they can in the last days of the final countdown of humanity.

A Rise in Apostasy

Apostasy is essentially the abandonment of one's personal religious faith. More specifically, the biblical references to the falling away of faith tend to be in regard to denying the Trinity of God or the belief that Jesus was both human and divine (1 John 2:22-23). And Scripture consistently warns of an increase of apostasy in the last days. (The "last days" can be technically defined as anytime after the life of Jesus [Hebrews 1:2], but the term is more frequently equated with the end times.)

We are told: "For [the coming again of our Lord Jesus Christ] will not come until there is a great rebellion against God and the man of lawlessness is revealed—the one who brings destruction" (2 Thessalonians 2:3). God is being patient with humanity, hoping that as many as possible will respond to His gracious offer of

TRIVIA TIDBIT

One reason Martin Luther got into such hot water during the Reformation was his writing that the Pope (Leo X) should be called Antichrist. Luther's complaint was that the church, by using Latin versions of Scripture that only a few specially educated people could understand, was guilty of impeding most citizens from understanding the gospel. He reasoned that such behavior was "antichrist." The Pope responded by calling Luther "the wild boar from the forest" who had a tongue like a fire.

SEE FOR YOURSELF

"[The second beast, or false prophet] required everyone—great and small, rich and poor, slave and free—to be given a mark on the right hand or on the forehead. And no one could buy or sell anything without that mark, which was either the name of the beast or the number representing his name. . . . Let the one who has understanding solve the number of the beast, for it is the number of a man. His number is 666" (Revelation 13:16-18).

SAYS WHO?

"Turning and turning in the widening
  gyre
The falcon cannot hear the falconer;
Things fall apart; the centre cannot hold;
Mere anarchy is loosed upon the world,
The blood-dimmed tide is loosed, and
  everywhere
The ceremony of innocence is drowned;
The best lack all conviction, while the
  worst
Are full of passionate intensity."
—*William Butler Yeats,* from "The Second
Coming"

salvation, so He postpones the final deadline for our benefit (2 Peter 3:8-9). But the longer Jesus waits to return, the more likely certain people are to use the delay as evidence that He's not coming back at all (2 Peter 3:3-4).

Most of today's Christians have dealt with apostasy of peers or family members. And as time goes by, apostasy is likely to spread.

A Run of the Millennium Theories

The Bible indicates quite clearly that all these events are to take place. Yet nowhere does it provide us with a timetable or even a definite sequence of events. Indeed, teachings about the last days are scattered throughout Scripture. The book of Revelation centers around that theme, but it uses many symbols and analogies that can be interpreted various ways. In addition, the information in Revelation is better understood when supported by valuable clues found in Daniel, Zephaniah, the teachings of Jesus and Paul, and other places. So it should not seem strange that when different Bible scholars study the bulk of material about the last days, they come up with divergent views of what to expect.

Let's start by taking a look at three traditional ways of interpreting the available information.

The Postmillennial Viewpoint

"Postmillennial" refers to the perception that the second coming of Jesus will take place *after* ("post") the 1000-year period spoken of in Revelation. And many postmillennialists suggest the thousand years is a generalization rather than a literal millennium—it might indeed be a much longer period of time.

The thinking is that as the gospel continues to spread, the world should become a much better place. At some point (which some people suggest was the first coming of Jesus, and others believe is yet in the future), the "millennium" will officially begin. During this time, the world will undergo a remarkable period of intense peace and righteousness. And after a thousand years (or so) of such vast improvement, then Jesus returns, at which time judgment and resurrection will take place.

From the postmillennial viewpoint, sin is not completely done away with during the millennium but is evident to a much lesser degree than in times past.

The Amillennial Viewpoint

The "a-" prefix indicates "against," such as in the words *amoral* or *atypical*. So the amillennial viewpoint is one that doesn't really endorse the millennium as a literal span of time. Amillennialists believe that both good and evil will continue to develop simultaneously until Jesus returns at the end of the world. At that time, we can expect judgment and resurrection. The biblical passages referring to the millennium are said to refer either to the current age where the church has a certain level of influence in the world, or to believers who have gone to heaven. But amillennialists are not expecting a specific thousand years or so when Jesus will rule on earth.

The beliefs of amillennialism are formulated by taking a less literal view of many key biblical passages—particularly prophecies which cannot be interpreted with absolute certainty. One of history's best-known amillennialists was Augustine. In his famous work, *City of God,* he wrote that the millennium would be the time between the first and second comings of Christ. That was thought to be the time when Satan was bound and the saints would reign with Jesus. Of course, Augustine lived from 354 until 430, so his theory could not be proved or disproved for over 500 years after he died. And indeed, there was considerable end-times speculation connected with the year 1000. But when Jesus didn't return at that time, amillennialists adopted a less literal interpretation of the 1,000-year length of time connected with the millennium.

The Premillennial Viewpoint

The premillennial view of the end times is based on a more literal interpretation of Scripture, and therefore can be a bit more complicated to understand and/or explain. The basic thinking is that the return of Jesus will take place *prior to* the millennium, and He will rule on earth for 1,000 years.

TRIVIA TIDBIT

In a 1993 poll conducted by *Time* and CNN, 20 percent of the adults who responded felt that the second coming of Jesus Christ would occur around the year 2000. Another 31 percent weren't sure. Only 49 percent responded with a definite no. This seems to indicate that, first of all, more people than we think might be giving some thought to the end times. And secondly, many seem to feel Jesus' return could be imminent.

Many proponents of premillennialism believe the great tribulation will be a seven-year period preceding the return of Jesus and His millennial kingdom. But they disagree more frequently about the rapture of the church. Some people strongly believe that Christians will suffer through the entire tribulation along with the rest of the world. Others believe just as strongly that God will remove believers before the worst comes to pass.

Arguments can be made that the rapture of the church might occur: (1) prior to the beginning of the great tribulation; (2) at the midpoint of the tribulation; or (3) at the end of the tribulation. Those who support one of the first two options must make allowances for more than one period of divine judgment and resurrection of the dead. If existing believers are instantly "raptured" (and therefore judged/rewarded) at one point, the nonbelievers therefore will not be judged until later. And assuming that some people will become believers during the great tribulation (even though it is likely to be a difficult choice to make under the circumstances), their rewards and resurrections will necessarily be later than the first batch of raptured believers.

Is There No End to End-times Speculation?

So the variables continue to multiply. Does Jesus come back before or after the millennium? Will there even be a literal 1,000-years? And if so, how does the great tribulation fit into the picture? Will the "rapture" of the church occur in time to prevent believers from suffering the horrendous ordeals described in Revelation, or will they have to endure the worst persecution in history? Believers have all sorts of speculations and expectations when it comes to the end times, and just because they tend to disagree doesn't mean one group is necessarily more spiritual than another.

To further complicate matters, many scholars go to great lengths to try to figure out how God will fulfill many of the promises He has made throughout Scripture. The Old Testament is filled with promises to the Jewish people—especially when it comes to specific cove-

nants with Abraham, David, and others. Many promises are also made to New Testament believers. As the wick of time burns down to the last remaining days on Planet Earth, those believing in the inerrancy of Scripture assume that all of God's promises will be fulfilled. So they search the Bible to find promises and then try to work them into the big puzzle of what's going to happen during the end times. And the more biblical references we compile about the last days, the less this puzzle seems like a jigsaw and the more it seems like a Rubik's cube.

But if we can learn to work on the puzzle regularly, without getting overly frustrated when we can't solve it right away, perhaps much of the confusion will clear up. If you have an interest in this area of Bible study, perhaps you should read a lot of varying opinions. See how each author stacks his or her presuppositions against what Scripture has to say. You aren't likely to completely agree with (or even understand) any single scholar. But you are likely to discover yourself thinking, *That makes sense* in some cases and, *That can't be right* in others.

A Sure Thing

In the meantime, don't get flustered if you don't understand it all. No one does! And just because we can't soak it all in and make sense of it, we shouldn't ignore it all, either. The book of Revelation, the record of all the end-times events John witnessed, was recorded to be sent out to various churches in order to encourage them and provide them with hope! For all the doom and gloom involved, the primary message is that God is always in control and will one day put a final end to all the sin and evil in the world. He will even put an end to the world, but only because He has something incredibly better in store for those who put their faith in Him.

As some people look into the future, all they see is Doomsday, so they respond with terror or overcompensate by shifting into party mode: Eat, drink, and be merry, for tomorrow we die. But believers see beyond the doom of the end times. For them, it is the final chapter in a history of sin and suffering. It's the turning point that

QUESTIONS?

Wouldn't it be more beneficial to forgo all the end-times speculation and focus on the clear truths of Scripture I can understand?

We certainly shouldn't spend more time speculating than in dealing with clear biblical truth. However, the Bible never seems to sidestep the topic of the last days. Therefore, it should be well worth our time to explore and meditate on the clear teachings of Scripture in regard to the end times. If it's in the Bible, we should assume it's there for a reason. Most Scripture begins as something of a mystery, but as we keep reading and thinking about it, many times we discover that God is a "revealer of mysteries" (Daniel 2:28-29).

TRIVIA TIDBIT

The big word for the branch of theology concerned with the end of the world is *eschatology*. It sounds somewhat like *eggs*-chatology, which is appropriate because some people have hard-boiled opinions in this area while others are over-easy. But truth be told, most of us have a somewhat scrambled understanding in this area of doctrine.

SAYS WHO?

"The church is always in danger of becoming Anti-Christ because it is not sufficiently eschatological. It lives too little by faith and hope and too much by the pretensions of its righteousness." —*Reinhold Niebuhr*

reunites them with God the way God intended things to be from the beginning.

We should certainly enjoy all the good things of the world while we can. Sure, we will face some down times. We will suffer because of the evil around us. We will have physical hurts and emotional scars. But God never deserts us, and He gives us the strength we need to overcome. And for those who overcome, incomprehensible wonders lie ahead.

As we struggle with all the confusing aspects of the end times, a few things should remain clear. First of all, the assurance of life after death keeps coming through. For those who belong to God, this is nothing but good news. And if we really believe this, then we can even learn to have a different perspective on life when things don't go as we wish. Our pains—even chronic, life-long pains—are only temporary! (2 Corinthians 4:16-18) In spite of such things, we can maintain a measure of hope and joy.

And realizing that judgment and reward lie ahead, we are also motivated to hold fast to the instructions of Scripture. The expectation of standing before God someday should encourage us to righteousness and purity. The theme of *believers* should be, "Eat, drink, and be holy, for tomorrow we live forever."

If we downplay the importance of end-times teachings, we might miss out on some realities that should inspire us throughout our lifetimes. But if we continue to struggle with understanding such things—muddled though our thinking might be—we will eventually come to some rewarding insights.

Questions to Ponder and/or Discuss

1. When you think about the end times, which of the following feelings do you experience?

Confusion	Despair	Depression	Joy
Hope	Confidence	Sadness	Terror
Anxiety	Remorse	Enthusiasm	Faith
Empathy for others	Spiritual zeal	Ambiguity	Apathy

   Other:

2. Which, if any, of the end-times scenarios make sense to you? What questions do you have about this period? What resources can you pursue (books, people, etc.) to find answers and additional information?

3. How do you think your spiritual life would be affected if you didn't know anything about the last days and end times? (Would you be better off? Would being kept in the dark be potentially harmful? Would it limit your understanding about God?)

Don't Know Much about (Church) History

The Church: Built on the Rock and on Rocky Ground Ever Since

A LOOK AT THE FIRST-CENTURY CHURCH

People who take up genealogy as a hobby are frequently surprised at what they find when they begin to trace their family history. Some people discover princesses, Nobel Prize winners, and heroes. Some uncover horse thieves, pirates, and politicians. And as researchers are confronted with both the mundane and the surprising, they generally piece together a more complete picture of the truth. (For example, perhaps Grandma's claim to nobility turns out to be her reign as Disco Queen of the Lower East Side.) Such revelations of the past—good or bad—are all helpful in understanding how a person became who he or she currently is.

A similar search can be beneficial in regard to the church. Many Christians today are faithful church attendees, biblically literate, and strong in their faith. Yet they have little if any comprehension of their spiritual "roots." We assume the church has a well-defined list of beliefs, and indeed, most denominations do. But we need to take a quick historical journey to discover how "the church" that

SOME THINGS YOU'LL DISCOVER IN THIS CHAPTER

1. How the church began

2. How the New Testament church differed from Old Testament worship models

3. Early threats to the newly-formed church

81

SAYS WHO?

"Study the past, if you would divine the future."—*Confucius*

arose at the death of Jesus has become the vast list of "churches" we find in the Yellow Pages. Only by doing so can we see how we have arrived at such a variety of doctrines and church practices. In addition, we will answer the question that keeps coming up: "Why don't all Christians believe the same things?"

Give Me That Old Testament Religion

From a biblical standpoint, we hear a lot about the formation of the church *after* Jesus' death. But prior to that we also find a couple of clues about where the church would be headed.

Prior to the New Testament church, God's people were well accustomed to group worship. As God was leading His people out of the slavery of Egypt, He provided them with specific blueprints and instructions for a tabernacle—a portable house of worship that contained among other things the ark of the covenant, the primary symbol of God's presence with His people.

After the Israelites arrived in the Promised Land, the people no longer moved as a single group but were divided into twelve tribes. The Levites, given no territory of their own, were instead planted among the other tribes to serve as priests and care for the religious development of the people. Worship began to be segmented to some extent as each tribe formed its own places to come together.

After the rise of David as king and a series of military victories and conquests, the nation of Israel pulled together again as its boundaries expanded. David established Jerusalem as the national capital and wanted to build a permanent temple there. But God determined that David's hands had shed too much blood and decreed that the temple would be built by David's son, Solomon, the next king.

Solomon's reign was marked by peace and prosperity, and he could devote himself to numerous building projects. But foremost among them was the temple described in 1 Kings 5–8. It wasn't particularly large, yet it was a magnificent building with expensive cedar paneling, much of it overlaid in gold and lavishly decorated.

The ark of the covenant was moved into a permanent Most Holy Place, where once a year the high priest would enter and make atonement for the sins of the people. And even though only priests were allowed to enter the temple, it was a symbol of how much God had done for His people.

And you probably know the rest of the story. After a short period of faithfulness to God, the people again forsook their loyalty to Him and turned to other gods. After a series of mostly corrupt and idolatrous kings, the divided kingdoms of Israel and Judah fell to the Babylonians and Assyrians.

Yet after a period of captivity, a remnant of God's people returned to their homeland with the permission of King Cyrus of Persia. A few Jews had been allowed to remain there, but the reunited Israelites were a meager number compared to what they had been in their glory days prior to captivity. Ezra and Nehemiah describe this period, during which the walls around Jerusalem were rebuilt, as was the temple. This project is frequently called "Zerubbabel's temple," named after one of the leaders during the return. No description of this temple is provided. Some scholars speculate it was built upon the same foundation as Solomon's temple, yet surely lacked much of the splendor of the previous house of worship.

TRIVIA TIDBIT

Solomon's temple was torched by the Babylonians in 587 B.C. So far, no remains have been found.

SAYS WHO?

"The Bible knows nothing of solitary religion."—*John Wesley*

To Hellenize and Back

Zerubbabel's temple was used until 168 B.C., when the Syrian king Antiochus IV (Epiphanes) robbed and desecrated it. Antiochus didn't just want to defeat the Jews; he wanted to "Hellenize" them—make them just like everyone else in an attempt to make the entire world one big Greek civilization. It would have pleased him to no end to do away with the Hebrew religion altogether. His brash actions initiated the Maccabean uprising.

In 165 B.C. a band of bold Jews, led by Judas Maccabaeus and his family, retook and cleansed the temple. While doing so, a meager supply of oil for the temple lamps burned for a miraculous length of time, which led to the annual Jewish celebration of Hanukkah.

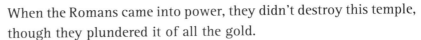

TRIVIA TIDBIT

Antiochus IV (Epiphanes) was a bad, bad man. He not only forbade Jewish worship and circumcision but also destroyed all the Hebrew writings he could find. And to show who was boss, he had a pig sacrificed on the altar of the temple in Jerusalem and dedicated the temple to Zeus.

SEE FOR YOURSELF

"Some of [Jesus'] disciples began talking about the beautiful stonework of the temple and the memorial decorations on the walls. But Jesus said, 'The time is coming when all these things will be so completely demolished that not one stone will be left on top of another'" (Luke 21:5-6).

When the Romans came into power, they didn't destroy this temple, though they plundered it of all the gold.

Somewhat later Herod the Great took it upon himself to give the temple a facelift as one of his many building projects on behalf of the Roman Empire (and his own legacy). And he probably hoped to win the support of the influential Jewish religious leaders who frowned upon his allegiance to Rome.

Herod's temple, as it came to be called at this point, was a beautiful building of gleaming white marble, with magnificent decorations, including gold panels on the eastern side to reflect the morning sunlight. A number of porches outside the temple itself allowed Gentiles and women to assemble. Otherwise these people were not allowed to participate in the religious ceremonies. The temple also had dozens of white marble Corinthian columns. The construction of the temple and surroundings was an ongoing project, taking decades to complete. But shortly after it was finished, war in Jerusalem led to its looting, burning, and destruction at the hands of Roman armies.

However, while the temple was important to the Jews and their ceremonies, they weren't completely dependent on it for spiritual growth and development. For one thing, not everyone could get to Jerusalem frequently. While the temple was a popular site for a pilgrimage or family vacation, not a large percentage of them could "go to church" there on a weekly basis.

During the captivity period, it is believed, the people had started meeting in small groups in localized geographic areas on their Sabbaths and religious holidays. From this tradition, many think, came the establishment of the local synagogue. While the temple was a place for group worship and offering sacrifices, the synagogue was an arena designed more for reading and discussing the Scriptures.

From the Temp-le to Something More Lasting

So by the middle of the first century, God's people were very familiar with temples and synagogues. Jesus Himself was known to visit the temple (at least once with whip in hand to toss out greedy merchants) and to speak in synagogues. But one day He turned to His disciples and asked who they thought He was. A lot of people had been speculating on this very topic, but Peter boldly replied, "You are the Messiah, the Son of the living God" (Matthew 16:16).

In response, Jesus said, "You are blessed, Simon son of John, because my Father in heaven has revealed this to you. You did not learn this from any human being. Now I say to you that you are Peter, and upon this rock I will build my church, and all the powers of hell will not conquer it" (Matthew 16:17-18). This is the first mention of *church* in the Bible, although the word Jesus used (meaning "assembly") is used in other places in reference to the congregation of Israel and to groups of Greek citizens within a city.

As Jesus directed the attention of His disciples toward the "church" He was building, He didn't promise just another synagogue, or even another temple. His concept of "church" seemed to be broader, more powerful, and completely new. It would be the assembly of *believers* rather than any particular structure.

From its very origin, the church seems to have been intended to be a cohesive "body," as we saw in Chapter 6. Jesus is the head, but all the other members need to learn to interact and work together without attempting to overshadow one another.

While there are only a few mentions of "church" in the Gospels, the term is used quite frequently in the book of Acts and the New Testament epistles. It soon becomes clear that the term "church" can mean both the totality of those who believe in Jesus Christ, as well as smaller specific bodies of believers. Therefore, when Paul addressed "the church at Corinth," he meant a specific local subgroup of the worldwide body of believers who happened to gather in a particular city in Greece.

These days Main Street Church of Christ and First Episcopal Church might be across the street from one another. As the two congregations file into their respective houses of worship, the members of one group may give the members of the other group funny looks or perhaps question some of the other church's specific doctrines. Yet in spite of meeting in separate buildings and

QUESTIONS?

What, exactly, was the "rock" that Jesus referred to in Matthew 16:18?

A case can be made for: 1) Jesus; 2) Peter's confession; or 3) Peter himself. We would certainly have no church without Jesus' sacrifice on our behalf. We could not be included in the body of believers without a heartfelt confession of faith in Jesus. And Paul later affirms that the church was "built on the foundation of the apostles and the prophets" (Ephesians 2:20). It is frequently pointed out that, in any event, Jesus seemed to be using a play on words between "Peter" (*petros*) and "rock" (*petra*).

SEE FOR YOURSELF

"All the believers were of one heart and mind, and they felt that what they owned was not their own; they shared everything they had. And the apostles gave powerful witness to the resurrection of the Lord Jesus, and God's great favor was upon them all. There was no poverty among them, because people who owned land or houses sold them and brought the money to the apostles to give to others in need" (Acts 4:32-35).

maintaining doctrinal variations, the members of both "churches" belong to the same "church" established by Jesus.

Before the Church Was Supersized

At one time the church had no such divisions as those mentioned above. The Bible gives a vivid description of a "church" the likes of which will probably never be seen again on earth. Everybody in the church jammed into a single building—most likely someone's home—to worship and learn from the mouths of the same apostles whose ears and minds had soaked in much of what Jesus had tried to teach them. The Holy Spirit was active among them, providing clear insight and direction. And the people were so committed to God and to one another that, in contrast, money and possessions meant little to them. If a person owned something someone else needed, it was given or sold to benefit the fellow church member(s).

A concise but clear picture of this first church is given at the end of Acts 4. However, the very next chapter of Acts introduces a couple whose motives were not pure, yet who tried to pass themselves off as fully devoted church members (and who were sentenced most severely for their attempted deception). Unfortunately, as the numbers of people began to grow, so did conflicts and divisions (Acts 5:1-11).

The church described in Acts 4:32-37 is a picture of fellowship and communion that many churches today attempt to emulate. Yet we can only begin to approach those conditions. Just as we can never have another first birthday, first date, first wedding anniversary, or first anything else, we will never again have another first church. Such is the toll of time and history.

Many of those people had known Jesus personally and had witnessed His miracles. They had heard not only His words but His voice inflections as well.

They were aware that He had left responsibility for the church in the hands of His apostles, and they didn't question the delegated authority. No pastor searches were required. When one person made a comment, every other person in the whole church heard it.

But this was a temporary condition. Jesus had made it clear that the mission of the church was to make disciples, baptize them into faith, and keep growing (Matthew 28:18-20).

Where's a Good Church Consultant When You Need One?

As the church spread, both because of growing numbers of believers and because of eventual persecution, the single *church* became plural *churches*. Almost immediately, problems arose. From within, the members of one local body bickered with members of another about who had the better church leadership (1 Corinthians 1:10-17). Needs arose that weren't being taken care of (Acts 6:1). And from without, various groups and power blocs tried to exert their influence over the newly forming congregations.

Even by the time Paul wrote his first letters to the new churches he had recently established, he was already being forced to address false teachings that were infiltrating the young congregations. One organized group exerting a damaging influence was known as the Judaizers. They were all for people becoming believers in Jesus, but they insisted that the new converts adhere to all the teachings of Judaism as well. The issue of circumcision was foremost among their concerns.

One of the first doctrinal crises of the Christian church was whether or not its members must be circumcised. Since all the prominent church leaders of the time were Jewish, you might think they would be inclined to endorse a circumcision mandate. Yet after witnessing the power of the Holy Spirit among the Gentiles who professed faith in Jesus, the church leadership ruled that Gentiles need not be circumcised as a prerequisite for becoming Christians (Acts 15:1-35).

Actually, the Judaizers expressed a valid concern. The Gentiles vastly outnumbered the Jews, and the Gentiles weren't known for their moral integrity. In fact, just the opposite was true of many of them. If hordes of unruly Gentiles were allowed to become Christians, some of the conscientious Jewish believers feared that the

QUESTIONS?

Why was God's judgment against Ananias and Sapphira (Acts 5:1-11) so harsh?

Had Ananias and Sapphira been honest about keeping some of the money, it would have been their right to do so. But they saw no harm in trying to "put one over" on the apostles. What they didn't realize was that lying to the new church leadership was tantamount to lying to God. And God made it clear that He was not capable of being deceived. This incident in the early church was a bold object lesson that God expected a higher standard from those professing faith in Him.

SAYS WHO?

"It is common for those that are farthest from God to boast themselves most of their being near to the Church."
—*Matthew Henry*

87

TRIVIA TIDBIT

A spin-off religion from Gnosticism taught that Jesus had only *seemed* to be flesh and blood and that in fact He had been a spirit the entire time. This belief came to be known as Docetism. (*Dokesis* is Greek for "appearance.")

Christian church would not (or perhaps *could* not) live up to the high moral standards set forth in the law of Moses. Yet in spite of these concerns the early church leaders refused to discriminate against Gentile believers.

Another group that seems to be rebutted in Paul's letters (though not addressed by name) was the Gnostic sect (from the Greek *gnosis*, meaning knowledge). The teachings of Gnosticism polarized spiritual things and physical things. The spirit was perceived as good; flesh (and other matter) was evil. Therefore, as their reasoning went, it was theoretically possible to sin up a storm in the flesh and still be all God wanted you to be, since God was only interested in the eternal spirit of the person.

The Gnostics also placed a high value on what they considered "special knowledge." In fact, this knowledge that was hidden from most people was more crucial to their belief system than the death and resurrection of Jesus. (After all, if Jesus was God incarnate—in the *flesh*—what could be the possible significance?)

Numerous New Testament writers addressed these and other heresies in their letters. Naturally, as the church continued to grow and influence greater numbers of people, it might be expected that the cultic offshoots of the church would increase as well.

Going outside the scriptural account into the historical one, we learn that other groups threatened the integrity of the new church. Most people know something about the plethora of Greek and Roman gods and goddesses that were regularly acknowledged during the first century. But other lesser known (yet equally influential) groups arose during this time, most of which were mystery religions. Some such religions are as follows:

Montanism (Named for its leader, Montanus)

Despite some quirky beliefs about how the kingdom of heaven would soon relocate to Asia Minor, the Montanists set some trends that cults throughout the centuries have copied, including:

- The claim to have a bold new revelation to add to the Bible
- Very charismatic individuals as leaders

- A stricter system of beliefs than those set forth by the Christian church
- The warning that to reject the teachings of Montanus was to reject "real" Christianity.

When it came to competing with genuine Christian faith and practice, the Montanists were onto something. Their techniques and teachings have worked for many cults since.

Mithraism (Named for "Mithras," the god of light in ancient Persia)

Again borrowing from Gnosticism, Mithraism taught that at death, the soul beamed out beyond the seven planets (all that were known at the time) to the spirit world. Only men were allowed into this sect, and many were soldiers. A big event when they met was sacrificing a bull.

Worship of Isis (The principal goddess of ancient Egypt)

As Roman soldiers ventured to Egypt and back, they were fascinated by much of what they saw there and quickly added Isis to their ever-growing pantheon of gods. Isis was worshiped as a nature goddess (mother and giver of life), and her influence came to rival even that of Juno.

Rock on!

Perhaps we're getting off track from our theme of "what Christians believe." However, we need to be aware of what the early Christians were up against. Clearly, some of these competing religions strayed far from the tenets of Christianity. Others, however, were only slightly off the mark, and these were probably more threatening to the average congregation of the time. The same is true of us today. You might tend to be a bit skeptical if an evangelist tries to convince you a spaceship is hiding behind a comet and will come to pick you up if you dress in purple shrouds and black Nikes and kill yourself. But when the next evangelist begins to preach on the financial benefits of Christianity at the exclusion of suffering, do your ears tend to perk up?

TRIVIA TIDBIT

After someone had worked his way to a certain level of devotion in Mithraism, a ceremony was held. The person stood beneath a platform onto which a bull was led. The animal was then slit open, allowing the blood to "baptize" the member.

SAYS WHO?

"It is right for the Church to be in the world; it is wrong for the world to be in the Church. A boat in water is good; that is what boats are for. However, water inside the boat causes it to sink." —Harold Lindsell

We've had 2,000 years of the formation of various groups that try to add to or alter the truth of what Christians believe. Most of them don't last very long, but a few have managed to do quite well. We'll continue to look at some of these groups in the next few chapters.

Many segments of Christianity remain rock solid in these trying times. But others, if we want to be truthful, sometimes find themselves on rather rocky ground. We will see that this is the pattern that has existed from the first church until today. But Jesus' promise is as valid now as it ever was: "Upon this rock I will build my church, and all the powers of hell will not conquer it" (Matthew 16:18).

Questions to Ponder and/or Discuss

1. In your spiritual experience, have you ever come across a church attempting to operate almost exactly as the first-century church did? What kind of success does (did) it have?

2. If you attend a church on a regular basis, in what ways do you think it is similar to the first-century church? In what ways has it "modernized" to accommodate for changing times?

3. What religious teachings or philosophies have you personally encountered that are contrary to Christian doctrines? How did you respond in each case? Have any of these outside influences infiltrated your church?

GROWTH OF THE CHURCH

Councils, Creeds, and Changes

CHURCH HISTORY:
THE FIRST 500 YEARS

SOME THINGS YOU'LL DISCOVER IN THIS CHAPTER

1. How the church responded to initial rapid growth

2. A rough timeline of events of the first 500 years of church history

3. An increased intensity of persecution of Christians

A long-standing principle of business is that it's a lot easier to start a company than to grow one. Each year many new businesses gear up, led by passionate, hard-working entrepreneurs who oversee the details of every aspect. Many times these new ventures have tremendous initial success, necessitating rapid growth. That's when the problems begin.

As the business takes on new levels of management or perhaps branches out with franchises, many new people are hired. Most are neither as passionate as the founders about the product nor as willing to work long hours. Communication becomes more difficult. Quality control breaks down. And before you know it, the new company that seemed to be going gangbusters has simply gone bust—financially and emotionally. It's a tricky business to grow at a rate fast enough to service all the new customers without compiling so much overhead that the end result ceases to be worth the effort.

91

Century One

The church isn't a business as such, yet it has faced many of the same problems and challenges in addressing the needs of its "customers" while growing in size for almost 2,000 years now. The first-century "start-up" was a tremendous success, as we have seen. Now we're going to look at a sketchy timeline of what took place during the first five centuries of church history.

The First Half of the First Century

We noted in the previous chapter that by the end of the first century, Paul was already having to rebut a number of doctrines that either directly opposed or subtly twisted the truth of Christianity. This was a trend that would continue. By the end of the second century, a Christian named Irenaeus had recorded 217 such "religions," and the 21st-century church continues to face a number of not-quite-right doctrines seeking to distort the truth.

All these varieties of religions would probably not have been much of a threat if the church had remained in Jerusalem and continued to be a united body. For a while it seemed that Christianity might have an easy road to success. Since it had come out of Judaism, it wasn't perceived as particularly threatening to the Romans. The Jews had already shown a lot of resistance to any attempts to "Hellenize" them—to impose upon them Greek culture, religion, and such. They wouldn't condone any emperor's claim to be divine, and they wouldn't even perform lip service to the numerous gods and goddesses of the Greeks and Romans.

But neither did they present any serious threat to the Roman Empire, so the two cultures had learned to coexist. The Jews were allowed to worship at the temple and attend their synagogues, and the Romans didn't hassle them too much. So when the Christian church sprang up, centered around a Jewish figure and led by Jewish believers, the Romans didn't discern much of a difference. Consequently, the church had considerable freedom at first.

But gradually that grace period came to a close. At first the main opponents of the church seemed to be certain powerful and influential Jewish leaders. Some of them had finagled the crucifixion of

NO-BRAINER'S GUIDE TO WHAT CHRISTIANS BELIEVE

Jesus and later attempted to impede the work of the apostles. They were also the ones who stoned Stephen to death, creating the first recognized Christian martyr (Acts 6:8–8:3). We are told that, "a great wave of persecution began that day" (Acts 8:1). The apostles remained headquartered in Jerusalem, but many of the other believers hightailed it into surrounding areas.

We know that Herod Antipas put to death John the Baptist and was involved in the trial of Jesus. His successor and nephew, Herod Agrippa I, killed James—the first apostle of Jesus to be put to death for his faith. When Herod saw how much James's death pleased the Jewish leaders, it motivated him to attempt further acts of persecution (Acts 12:1-4). And things were only going to get worse.

The Jerusalem Council (A.D. 48 or 49)

A council was held in Jerusalem where church leaders discussed the problems that were arising because of the conversion of Gentiles. (This meeting was mentioned in the previous chapter.) The agenda and "minutes" of this meeting are described in Acts 15. Paul and Barnabas had just returned from their first journey where they had made contact with several of the newly formed churches, so they were welcomed as guest speakers.

It was a crucial debate. Some of the new believers (they weren't being called "Christians" quite yet) had been high-ranking Jewish officials. Others were Gentiles who had little if any religious training and might not even have had basic reading skills. Those with a traditional Jewish background were uncomfortable with opening church membership to people who had little if any comprehension of Jewish law and ethics. But the council could not dispute the testimony of Paul and Barnabas that the Holy Spirit was definitely at work among the Gentile believers as well as the Jewish ones. The final ruling of the council was that circumcision was not a requirement for church members.

Although strong opinions were held for both points of view, this controversial issue didn't split the church. The first big test was passed with flying colors.

QUESTIONS?

With all the persecution in Jerusalem, why didn't everyone pack up and move to a safer place?

The persecution that scattered believers throughout the lands is frequently perceived to be part of God's plan to send the Gospel beyond the city limits of Jerusalem and into the rest of the world. Yet Jerusalem was, and still is, a treasured city for the Christians and Muslims, as well as the Jews. It was the place to be because it was a crossroads for people from everywhere in the surrounding communities. The temple made it a center of religion as well. In addition, persecution was nothing new to this culture, and the now-strong apostles were willing to endure it—no matter what the consequences.

A historian named Tacitus wrote of Christian persecution: "Their death was made a matter of sport; they were covered in wild beast's skins and torn to pieces by dogs; or were fastened to crosses and set on fire in order to serve as torches by night. . . . Nero had offered his gardens for the spectacle and gave an exhibition in his circus, mingling with the crowd in the guise of a charioteer or mounted on his chariot. Hence, . . . there arose a feeling of pity, because it was felt that they were being sacrificed not for the common good, but to gratify the savagery of one man."

The Big Fire of Rome (A.D. 64)

As we have said, for several decades the new Christian church enjoyed much freedom because of its Jewish ties. Yet now in its adolescence, it was beginning to experience some growing pains. Not exactly Jewish, and by no means secular, the church began to feel a bit of persecution from both sides. Out of this persecution they would be forced to establish their own identity.

By the time of Nero's reign when a great fire destroyed much of Rome, the Christian segment was merely a hanging chad on the ballot that was Judaism. Some suggest Nero personally ordered the fire, but evidence is inconclusive. Regardless of what actually happened, the Christians—not the Jews—got the blame. Persecution against them began to intensify.

Destruction of Herod's temple (A.D. 70)

When it comes to politics and social concerns, any significant group of people are going to have diverse opinions. (Oil lobbyists and Greenpeace volunteers might all be Texans, for example, but that's where the similarities end.) This was true of the first-century Jews. Some were pacifists; others were more radical. But at one point the militant segment took action and pushed the Romans too far.

This conflict escalated over decades, but one of the first dramatic events was a Roman siege of Jerusalem in A.D. 70. The Jews trapped in the city faced great suffering from April until September, when the city fell at last. And as the Roman soldiers stormed in, they looted and leveled the temple.

The destruction of the temple forced the Jews out of the city and into various scattered synagogues for their worship. Gentiles could sit in to learn the Scriptures and perhaps develop some basic reading skills from the better-educated Jews. (Gentile involvement at the temple had been limited.) In addition, a lot of Gentiles were jaded with the impersonal and numerous Greek and Roman deities. The concept of not only a monotheistic religion, but also one where God actually cared what happened to His people, was quite appealing to many of them. And when the Christian church started to break away from its Jewish roots, the churches formed much along the lines of the synagogues, and many Gentiles began to join. So even though the temple was a prime Jewish symbol, its fall had an effect on the Christian church.

SEE FOR YOURSELF

Centuries Two through Five

It didn't take long for the church to develop something of an identity crisis. It was no longer exactly Jewish; on the contrary, it soon became predominately Gentile. The apostles who had been left in charge were dying off from various causes—mostly beheadings, crucifixion, and the like.

The single church "body" formed in Jerusalem had quickly become dozens or hundreds of localized "bodies," with numerous local pastors and/or traveling preachers who checked in only occasionally. Various questionable doctrines were being promoted—some seeking to keep Christianity tied to Judaism and others attempting to blend it too heavily into paganism. What was a young new church to do?!

It had been so easy (though they hadn't realized it) when Jesus was leading the way and all everyone else had to do was tag along and listen. And even with the apostles taking over, the transition had been a smooth and natural one. But now, with the ever-changing political climate, the deployment from Judaism, the ongoing persecution, and the numerous threats of heresy, the church needed a plan.

The first part of the plan required a firm determination about what, exactly, they believed. With all the various teachings attempting to leech into church doctrine, the church needed to determine which writings were truly inspired by God and which weren't. Next, they needed to decide who would be in charge of things now that the apostles were no longer around.

Creation of the Canon

The word *canon* comes from the Greek word *kanon*, meaning "measuring rule." So the "canon" of Scripture is the collection of individual writings that have become the standard we know as the Bible.

Herod's temple wasn't completed until A.D. 64, and it was utterly destroyed in A.D. 70. But the destruction shouldn't have come as a surprise to anyone who had been paying attention to Jesus:

"Do you see all these buildings? I assure you, they will be so completely demolished that not one stone will be left on top of another!" (Matthew 24:2).

Why are the Protestant and Catholic canons different?

As late as 1545, certain writings whose authenticity had been debated for centuries were still being considered for addition to the official canon. The Protestant "reformers" rejected these additional books, largely because New Testament writers never made reference to them. And perhaps as a reaction against the Protestants as much as anything, the Catholic Church endorsed them. So the Catholic canon includes the Apocrypha (or the "deuterocanonical" books), while the Protestant canon doesn't.

The determination of what to include began almost as soon as some of the works were written. Just as the New Testament writers already had a body of work established as "the law and the prophets" (essentially our Old Testament), they realized that significant writings about Jesus would need to be added.

By about A.D. 144, a canon of Christian writings had appeared. By A.D. 200 the collection had become essentially the same as our existing New Testament. The four Gospels, the historical book of Acts, and the writings of Paul were (almost) universally accepted immediately. Some of the other books received a bit more debate but were soon included. And by A.D. 397, the Christian church, for the most part, had finalized its canon.

In determining the original canon of what to include or exclude, several factors were considered, including:

- *The authority of the writing itself.* Since "all Scripture is inspired by God" (2 Timothy 3:16), any clear message of God to His people was a prime factor in including it among the books of Scripture.
- *Endorsement of human authorities.* The modern world is accustomed to expecting hoaxes when it comes to potentially valuable documents. (Recent years have turned up fakes of Hitler's diaries and Howard Hughes's will, to name just a couple of examples.) The ancient world also had its share of writers who would like to have had their writings published as being as authoritative as Scripture, even though they weren't. So the canon of Scripture was closely examined, questioned, debated, and eventually approved by numerous official councils before anything got into our Bible.
- *Clear statements by human authors.* Paul made it clear that he was writing as a designated apostle of Jesus (1 Corinthians 9:1-2; 2 Corinthians 14:37). Peter also endorsed the writings of Paul as being "the wisdom God gave him" (2 Peter 3:15-16). Other New Testament writers appeared to quote from one another in places. And in certain spots, such as John's writing in Revelation, the authors made it clear that readers should not

add to nor take away from what was being said (Revelation 22:18-19).

The early church had no qualms about accepting what the eyewitnesses to Jesus' teachings had to say. In addition, Jesus had foretold that one of the roles of the Holy Spirit would be to "guide you into all truth" (John 16:12). As the Holy Spirit moved certain people to record the gospel of Jesus, the history of the church, instructions for Christian living or church leadership, or anything else, those writings were accepted by the first-century believers and Christians ever since.

Every so often a cult or religious splinter group attempts to introduce "new" divinely inspired writings to add to the Bible. But the Christian church considers the matter closed. God has provided us with what we need to know, and the Holy Spirit is at work to help us understand and apply those teachings. We are not to accept extrabiblical writings as being inspired—at least, not on the same level as the Bible.

Increased Authority of Church Leaders

So rather than being dependent on oral tradition, Christianity based its authority on the Word of God and wrote down the official version in black and white. Yet with the spread of alternative doctrines and spurious writings also attempting to pass themselves off as inspired, the need arose for people to speak with authority on behalf of God and truth—to endorse the written Word as being legitimate and sacred.

As time passed, the original eyewitnesses to Jesus died off, leaving the job of teaching and training to others. The rise of "bishops" (church overseers) is viewed differently through Protestant and Catholic lenses. Both groups concur that strong leadership was needed to teach new converts, rebut and reject the false teachings that threatened the church, maintain church order, administer the sacraments, and so forth. But in general the Catholics feel the leadership roles were to be filled by those designated by the original apostles, the next openings filled by those who had been previously

SAYS WHO?

"Forasmuch as some have taken in hand, to reduce into order for themselves the books termed apocryphal, and to mix them up with the divinely inspired Scripture . . . it seemed good to me also . . . to set before you the books included in the Canon, and handed down, and accredited as Divine. . . . These are fountains of salvation, that they who thirst may be satisfied with the living words they contain. In these alone is proclaimed the doctrine of godliness. Let no man add to these, neither let him take aught from these."—*Athanasius (Bishop of Alexandria, A.D. 367)*

TRIVIA TIDBIT

Here are a couple of snippets from writers involved with the early church:

- "Follow the presbytery [in other words, the elders or priests] as Jesus Christ followed the Father."—Ignatius, A.D. 112

- "The bishop is in the Church and the Church in the bishop, and that if anyone be not with the bishop he is not in the Church"—*Cyprian (Bishop of Carthage, early to mid-200s)*

chosen, and so forth. Most Protestants aren't so convinced of the importance of "apostolic succession."

Such differences of opinion are due in part to the lack of historic detail in regard to first-century and second-century church life. Paul had provided a number of guidelines for choosing qualified church leaders, but nowhere in the New Testament do we find a detailed organizational chart for how the church should be set up.

As sketchy as the details are for this early period of the church, many of the available writings during that time reflected the dangers of heresy and the need for church-based interpretation of truth. It seems logical that during this time the tradition arose of having a single bishop take primary authority for each individual church. In this role, the idea was that he would be "first among equals" in regard to other church officials, yet the title of bishop has certainly carried with it a lot of power during periods of church history.

Increased Persecution

Believers needed the assurance of God's promises to them because the early persecution of the church was nothing compared to what followed in the second and third centuries A.D. Prior to the year 300, more Christians died at the hands of their fellow community members than from any kind of government mandate.

Much of the early persecution of the church took place because of misunderstandings. To the Romans, Christians were considered atheists because they refused to pledge allegiance to any Roman deities. Christian references to partaking of the "body and blood of Christ" led others to think they practiced cannibalism in their services. All the talk of love led to additional speculation concerning orgies, incest, and other misguided claims.

For a while the levels of persecution varied with the degree of interest the current Roman leader had with Christianity. Some of the rulers' family members, if not the leaders themselves, were being influence by the Gospel; others weren't. Meanwhile, Christians were becoming viable members of society to the extent they were able, including service in the Roman armies.

In the year 300, the primary emperor of Rome was Diocletian. He had divided the empire into four jurisdictions, appointing a ruler over each segment while remaining in power over them. Diocletian had ties to Christianity, perhaps through his wife and daughter. But he also saw Christianity as a potential source of division in his empire. In addition, one of the "junior emperors" named Galerius was quite hostile toward those involved in the relatively new religion.

In an attempt to remove Christians from the fighting ranks, laws were passed requiring soldiers to offer sacrifices to the gods, with death for those who refused. This put Christian soldiers in a dilemma. Within three years Galerius had stepped up his attack by decreeing that Christian writings and places of worship be destroyed. At first Diocletian forbade any executions, but the senior emperor's declining health eventually allowed Galerius to act with impunity. Christians faced harsh persecution, and thousands of deaths ensued. In some geographic areas, Christianity disappeared altogether.

But Galerius wasn't as tough as he thought he was. When dying (perhaps from stomach cancer), he revoked the laws that threatened Christianity and asked Christians to pray for him.

SAYS WHO?

"There is no greater drama in human record than the sight of a few Christians, scorned or oppressed by a succession of emperors, bearing all trials with a fierce tenacity, multiplying quietly, building order while their enemies generated chaos, fighting the sword with the word, brutality with hope, and at last defeating the strongest state that history has known. Caesar and Christ had met in the arena, and Christ had won."—*Will Durant*

Martyrs of the Early Church

Below are a few of the better known martyrs in the early church. There were many, many others, of course.

- Clement of Rome, thought to have been tied to an anchor and tossed into the sea in A.D. 101 or 100.
- Ignatius, bishop of Antioch in Syria, who died in the arena in 110.
- Polycarp was sentenced to be burned at the stake in 156. According to *Foxe's Book of Martyrs*, his body wouldn't burn as he sang amid the flames, so he was speared until he lost so much blood that the fire was extinguished, as was his life.
- Justin Martyr defended Christians against several false accusations being leveled against them. For his efforts he was labeled a subversive and put to death in 165.

TRIVIA TIDBIT

The first Nicene Council had connections to both Santa Claus and Turkey. It is thought that Santa Claus was in attendance. Back then, however, he was called St. Nicholas of Myra in Lycia—located in modern-day Turkey.

- Perpetua was a young woman who refused to renounce her Christian beliefs when commanded to do so. Her journal, one of the few surviving ancient works written by a female, conveys her thoughts up to her execution (by sword) in 203.
- Erasmus (St. Elmo) was an early Christian bishop martyred around 303 under the persecution of Diocletian.

Constantine and the Councils at Nicaea (A.D. 325 and 381)

The westernmost area of Diocletian's reign had been assigned to a man named Constantius Chlorus, the father of a leader named Constantine. After the death of Diocletian, the various leaders began to struggle for primary leadership. After a dozen years or so, Constantine finally emerged as the sole emperor in 324. He attributed his success to a vision he had of a cross of light above the sun, with a sign attached reading, "Conquer by this." He soon legalized Christianity and tolerated other religions that were peaceful.

Whether or not Constantine was "converted" as we use the word is debated. Some people consider his faith as genuine and legitimate. Others suggest he saw in Christianity an opportunity to unite his followers.

Regardless of his intentions, the church found itself in an unprecedented time of peace and acceptance. It wasn't long before Constantine sponsored the first worldwide church conference, attended by about 230 bishops from throughout the empire. Constantine might have been attempting to curry favor, but still the timing was good for a church get-together.

Now almost three centuries after the crucifixion and resurrection of Jesus, the church was still trying to figure out all the theology about who He was. A prominent figure named Arius had begun in 318 to promote the idea that Jesus was not quite on the same status level as God the Father. His thinking was that God the Father was not created but had always existed. Jesus, however, had been born just like all the other beings created by the Father. So no matter how highly the church held Jesus, He would never deserve exactly the same glory due God.

Questions concerning the nature and divine position of Jesus had been debated throughout church history. But it was at this point that both Constantine and the church leaders wanted to reach a consensus. If people were putting faith in Jesus as the source of salvation, yet He wasn't exactly God, what did that mean to the church?

To rebut Arius arose a man name Athanasius. His reasoning was that Jesus had to be every bit as much God as God the Father in order to effect salvation for humanity. He argued that Jesus was "begotten" by God, not created in the same manner as the rest of us creatures. And, in a crucial distinction arising from Nicaea, Athanasius determined that Jesus was "of one substance" with the Father. In describing this, he used a Greek word (*homoousios*) which was a philosophical term not found anywhere in Scripture. But better than anything else it expressed the thought that Jesus was every bit as much God as the Father (and for that matter, so was the Holy Spirit).

The council drafted a creed to express the truths they agreed on. Although the logic and reasoning of Athanasius made sense to most of the representatives at Nicaea, Arius still had his supporters. And since this was new spiritual terrain for them, the council adjourned to think about what they had discussed.

In 381, a second council of Nicaea was called. By this time, most of the representatives were comfortable with what they had previously determined, and they reworded the Nicene Creed to be a bit more specific. Many churches continue to use this creed, now over 1600 years old.

The councils at Nicaea were significant for a number of reasons. To begin with, they succeeded in achieving a uniformity of thought for what church members were expected to believe. In addition, it was the first major cooperative effort between the church and big government. Never before had an empire taken such an interest in Christianity. And finally, the councils set a precedent for using Greek philosophical terms to apply to church theology. Each of these points was a potential cause of concern, but with the ongoing expansion of Christianity, most of the representatives saw the need for hashing through all these issues.

TRIVIA TIDBIT

One of the primary dissenters at Chalcedon was a man named Nestorius. He readily acknowledged the deity of Jesus, yet wasn't convinced by those who argued that Jesus had two natures within a single person. Nestorius also opposed the growing veneration/worship of Mary, which placed him again in the minority. Eventually Nestorius not only lost the debate but was even excommunicated. Still, he retained a following, and a group of believers called the Monophysites ("*one-nature*," to reflect the idea that Jesus had one nature rather than two) has existed ever since. The Coptic church in Egypt still maintains Nestorian beliefs.

The Council of Chalcedon (A.D. 451)

As religious people pondered the results of the councils of Nicaea, many were soon scratching their heads. They had all basically agreed that Jesus was God every bit as much as God the Father. Yet Jesus had also been human. So questions kept popping up about the nature (or was it *natures?*) of Jesus. It was a perplexing concept.

To address this issue, the new emperor Marcian borrowed from Constantine's strategy and called together a council, this time at Chalcedon, which was near Constantinople. The council dealt with some tough questions:

- When the "Word" became flesh, was God's nature potentially changed, weakened, or threatened?
- Did Jesus have the body of a person and the soul of God?
- Did Mary give birth to "God" or to the human Jesus?
- Did the human and divine natures of Jesus work at odds with one another, creating a sort of spiritual schizophrenia?

We can't get into the whole debate here, but the result of all the discussion was a basic agreement that Jesus was one person consisting of two natures. Each of His two natures—the human and the divine—"carries on its proper activities in communion with the other."

Not everyone could agree, and certain representatives began to pull away from the group to continue to promote their dissenting opinions. As we will see in the next chapter, this was only the first of many church divisions yet to come.

Church Committee Members Feel Their Pain

If you relate to the old song that begins, "Don't know much about history," then this chapter (and the next couple) may seem like Greek to you. Yet the contemporary church owes much to the people who first set out to do some heavy theological thinking. It's a simple matter for us to grab a commentary or Bible dictionary off the shelf and see what we ought to think about the nature of Jesus, His humanity, His divine aspects, and so forth. But consider what it must have been like to write the first drafts of such deep spiritual matters.

The church of the 300s, 400s, and 500s had come a long way from meeting in a single room "as one" and talking about the good old days when Jesus had walked among them. Jesus was just as vital to these later centuries of church life, yet they were being forced to think of Him in new ways.

We can hardly do justice to 500 years of history in a single chapter, but we're going to try to cover *twice* as much time in the next chapter. If you still have questions about people and/or events, be assured that plenty of good resource material exists. If you wish to plow ahead, go to it. If, however, you want to conduct some further research at this point, stop for a while and consult some good references on church history. The rest of this book will still be there when you're ready.

Key Church Leaders of the First 500 Years

Here are just a few more of the people and events that were important to the time period covered in this chapter.

- Tertullian (160–225) served as a wise and witty defender of Christians and their faith. Late in life, however, he lost the support of many when he joined the Montanist movement.
- Origen (185–254) was a legendary teacher and immensely prolific writer.
- John Chrysostom (347–407) earned his last name ("golden-mouthed") because of his clear preaching and personal application of Scripture.
- Jerome (347–419?) was a serious Christian scholar commissioned by the pope to translate the Greek and Hebrew Scriptures into Latin so that "regular" people could have access to them. His translation of the Bible is known as the Vulgate.
- Patrick was a British teenager when Irish raiders invaded his village sometime in the fifth century and took him a slave to Ireland. He eventually escaped, but later returned voluntarily to teach unbelievers about Christ. He has since become quite a popular and legendary figure.

103

Questions to Ponder and/or Discuss

1. How do you think you would have fared during this phase of church history? What do you think might have been your biggest concern? Do you think you would have been willing to die for what you believed?

2. On a scale of 1 (least) to 10 (most), how complete is your knowledge of church history? Which of the people named in this chapter are most familiar to you? Which, if any, of the names are new or vague? (If time permits, make a list and do a little additional research into the lives of these faithful people.)

3. If asked to define what you believe as simply as possible, what would you say? Without consulting any other sources, see how well you can do at writing your personal creed. (Until you give it a shot, it's difficult to appreciate all the hard work of others.)

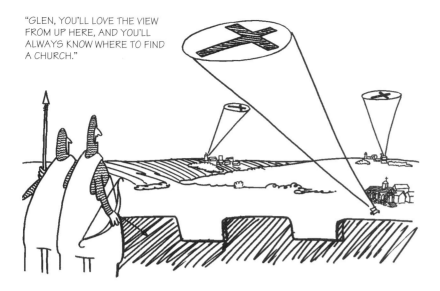

CHAPTER TEN

"GLEN, YOU'LL LOVE THE VIEW FROM UP HERE, AND YOU'LL ALWAYS KNOW WHERE TO FIND A CHURCH."

Light in the Dark Ages
Church History from A.D. 500 to 1500

Irreconcilable differences.

It's a phrase that's all too common in modern culture, used particularly in association with divorce. Sometimes a marriage lasts for decades, strong and seemingly unshakable. But then, for some reason, the couple drifts apart to the point where they desire an official dissolution. There's no abuse. No mental anguish. Perhaps not so much as an argument about who is more at fault. Nothing "big" to cite as the reason. But those two words, "irreconcilable differences," are enough to justify the permanent split.

As we follow the history of the church from where we left off in the last chapter, prepare yourself. Much of what we will witness is not a pretty sight. The church is beginning to fracture, on its way to certain splits for clear political or theological reasons. Yet sometimes the basic cause boils down to "irreconcilable differences."

As a result of 2,000 years of the church dividing and subdividing like a randy amoeba, many of us have learned to express skepticism and suspicion about the segments of the church we've separated

SOME THINGS YOU'LL DISCOVER IN THIS CHAPTER

1. Why church splits aren't necessarily a bad thing

2. The Crusades, the bubonic plague, the great schism, and other challenges for the church

3. A few positive things taking place during the Middle Ages

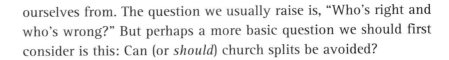

SAYS WHO?

"We know what happens to people who stay in the middle of the road. They get run over."—*Aneurin Bevan*

SEE FOR YOURSELF

The details of Paul and Barnabas's first journey are found in Acts 13–14. The two were so impressive in their delivery of the gospel that they were even thought to be "gods in human bodies" at one point (Acts 14:11-13).

ourselves from. The question we usually raise is, "Who's right and who's wrong?" But perhaps a more basic question we should first consider is this: Can (or *should*) church splits be avoided?

The First Band to Break Up after Going on the Road?

Let's think back for a moment to one of the first major rifts in the life of the church. The church leadership had already dealt with complaints about discrimination in the ministries of the church (Acts 6:1-2) and was gearing up for a major debate on whether Gentiles would need to be circumcised prior to church membership (Acts 15). Both of these delicate issues were handled with wisdom and diplomacy, and the church grew even stronger as a result.

Meanwhile, persecution had sent believers scattering from their all-in-one-accord commune in Jerusalem to various surrounding areas. The leaders decided that Paul and Barnabas should visit and encourage some of the newly forming churches outside of Jerusalem.

God's will for these two men couldn't have been clearer. They were singled out by the Holy Spirit for this specific task. They fasted and prayed in preparation for their journey. The church leaders placed their hands on them and sent them out with their blessing. And their journey was successful as they faithfully preached the good news, made new disciples, and spiritually strengthened those who were already believers.

Yet after Paul and Barnabas returned from their first journey and began to plan a second one, a major conflict arose. On the first trip they had taken a young relative of Barnabas's, named John Mark. But the young Mark had bailed out on them before they had gone very far. Barnabas was eager to give Mark another chance, but Paul didn't think it prudent.

This doesn't seem like such a terrible problem, yet Paul and Barnabas "had such a sharp disagreement that they parted company" (Acts 15:39). Barnabas paired up with John Mark and went one direction. Paul drafted a new partner named Silas and went another.

So who was right in the Paul vs. Barnabas conflict? We can certainly understand Paul's desire to cut any dead weight from his traveling crew. He was a pastor/evangelist/consultant/road warrior. He didn't have time to be a baby-sitter as well. With all their physical and spiritual challenges, Paul had little tolerance for the complaints of a young whiner: "I'm tired. I want to go home. If I have to eat camelburgers again tonight, I'm gonna hurl. Wah, wah, wah."

So does that mean Barnabas was wrong? What would have been the message to John Mark if Barnabas had left him behind and taken off with Paul again: one mistake in life and you're a permanent loser? Was it such a bad idea for Barnabas to take Mark under his wing and let him develop into a vibrant spiritual leader in his own time, and not according to Paul's timetable?

The biblical account doesn't take sides in this division. We are told that Paul and Silas had success in their continued travels to keep the various local churches going strong. And we learn that, after the tutelage of Barnabas, John Mark became a worthy disciple. In fact, Paul later sent for him specifically.

Not only did Mark become valuable to Paul, who had originally rejected him, but he also wrote the Gospel of Mark. Thanks to the patience and encouragement of Barnabas, young John Mark made a major contribution to Christian history that continues to influence believers today.

So in the original conflict, who was more correct: Paul or Barnabas? Even though they were both tremendous men of God, personally selected by the Holy Spirit and endorsed by the entire church body, they had a conflict that led to a split. And because they both were committed to what they thought was the right thing to do, *both* of them brought about positive change for generations to follow.

What can we learn from this biblical account? Perhaps one lesson is that certain church splits are unavoidable and perhaps even necessary at times. At the very least, let's not assume that every single conflict and/or split is due to one or both parties being wrong, arrogant, or out of God's will. Sometimes, of course, this may be the case—but not always.

SEE FOR YOURSELF

Either John Mark made some major changes, or Paul had a big change of heart. In Paul's later life, he wrote: "Only Luke is with me. Bring Mark with you when you come, for he will be helpful to me" (2 Timothy 4:11).

TRIVIA TIDBIT

The phrase, "When in Rome, do as the Romans do," may have had a Christian origin. In one of St. Augustine's letters, he wrote, "My mother, having joined me at Milan, found that the church there did not fast on Saturdays as at Rome, and was at a loss what to do. I consulted St. Ambrose, of holy memory, who replied, 'When I am at Rome, I fast on a Saturday; when I am at Milan, I do not. Follow the custom of the church where you are.'" Later writers seem to have paraphrased Ambrose's advice.

Going through a Middle Ages Crisis

A recent tendency has been to call the Middle Ages the Dark Ages, but let's not be too quick to turn out the lights on 1,000 years of history (approximately A.D. 500 to 1500). This time period comprises more than half of the existence of the church, so let's hope *something* was going on. The church during this time frequently gets a bad rep. But consider that today, if Jerry Springer had a choice of featuring a priest who has faithfully modeled the grace of God for fifty years or a pastor who once had a sexual affair with his secretary, which one do you think would get the air time for Tuesday's show? Similarly, we may hear more about the church's faults during the Middle Ages than its good points.

The Fall of the Roman Empire (Fourth and Fifth Century)

Part of the darkness of these ages was intellectual. The Roman Empire fell to various wild and woolly tribes (Huns, Vandals, Vikings, Visigoths, etc.). The city of Rome was sacked, and the vast geographic area that had been "Rome" was divvied up by the warring tribes. The roads and other grand projects that endured the overthrow soon deteriorated due to lack of upkeep. People didn't travel as much, and rural life became the norm. The great thinkers of Greece and Rome became distant memories. In fact, the *church* came to be known (for a while, at least) as the place to go if you were looking for intellectuals.

The Spread of Islam (A.D. 600 and onward)

As the Christian church was faltering a bit during the Middle Ages, the new religion of Islam began to spread rapidly, moving westward from Arabia and up across the Mediterranean from Northern Africa. Mohammed, born in 570, had quite a following by the early 600s. And Islam didn't spread because its pacifistic disciples handed out tracts in airports. Instead, Muslim armies conquered new territory, and the losers were expected to convert.

Conquered people who wished to maintain their Christianity could do so but had to pay extra taxes and identify themselves through clothing and/or badges. They were also forbidden to build new churches, and attempting to evangelize Muslims was at times punishable by death. Christianity disappeared in several geographic locations as Islam spread through Northern Africa, Spain, and France. In other places, such as Egypt, the Christian church has struggled as a minority presence from then until now.

Islam vs. Christianity

- Islam emphasizes one God at the expense of acknowledging the deity of Jesus.
- Muslims respect a number of prophets, including Adam, Noah, Abraham, Moses, and Jesus. But Mohammed, the founder of the religion, is more highly revered as the final and finest of God's messengers.
- God is perceived as less personal and more judgmental.
- Salvation is a matter of working for God rather than receiving His forgiveness by grace.

Yet as with many other religions, the small percentage of militant Muslims gets more than its share of attention. Many Muslims are quite devout and dedicated. In places where Islam has become the established religion, it has frequently had an overall positive influence on the communities. In recent years, it has been the world's fastest-growing religion.

Constantinople continued as a prominent center of Christianity for almost 1,000 years after the fall of the Roman Empire, but it finally lost its Christian status after the Islamic Turkish armies showed up and took over in 1453. From that point onward, Rome was recognized as the seat of the Christian church. Further efforts to grow, having met firm resistance from Muslim armies to the east, were directed north into Europe instead.

The "Great Schism" (1054)

In time, problems arose with the continuity of the church. The center of the church had been in Rome, but now the second, growing center in Constantinople was dividing loyalties of believers. Rome had maintained Latin as its official language; those in Constantinople

TRIVIA TIDBIT

Language students speculate that our word *roam* might derive from the city of Rome, which was a popular destination for pilgrims during the Middle Ages. Definite proof is hard to come by, although the word for "pilgrim" or "wanderer" is *romier* in French, *romero* in Spanish, and *romeo* in Italian.

spoke Greek. When councils were held in Constantinople, they were naturally much more heavily attended by church leaders from the East than from Rome. The East was more accustomed to philosophical speculation; the West tended to set more logical, precise standards for what was to be accepted or rejected. Consequently, communication between the two religious centers was frequently strained.

For hundreds of years, the church tried to resolve the differences and controversies that inevitably arose because of the twin centers of influence and the distance between them. In addition to theological disagreements, the politics involved made reconciliation impossible. Finally, in 1054, the East and West agreed to disagree, and they split for good in what has been labeled "the Great Schism." In spite of a couple of well-meaning attempts to get back together in later centuries, the Orthodox Church of the East has been somewhat isolated since that time.

The Crusades (1096–1272)

In the category of "It sounded like a good idea at the time," we have the Crusades. At a religious rally in Clermont, France, in 1095, Pope Urban II announced it was God's will to release the Holy Land from the influence of Islam. The Eastern emperor had enlisted his help, and he was more than willing to respond. Europe during this time had become a military hotbed with knights and soldiers perpetually looking for action. The pope was finding it difficult to enforce peace with all the rowdies congregated at the same place. It seemed a good idea for both East and West to send the action-ready soldiers on the road to combat a common enemy.

The first Crusade succeeded in recapturing Jerusalem in 1099, but the crusaders weren't picky about who they killed. Muslim soldiers died, but so did Jews and Arab Christians. Far too many people died because of the way they looked. And things went downhill from there.

Perhaps some of those in the army truly believed they were fighting for God and country, yet others had different motives. By the fourth Crusade (1202–1204), the European crusaders had lost any

vestige of holiness or nobility. Like college students on spring break, they poured into Constantinople and trashed the city that was supposedly their ally. For 900 years the municipality had been a center of influence, with art and culture of its own in addition to a large collection of many of the great treasures of ancient Greece. But the crusaders grabbed whatever they could for themselves and destroyed most of the rest. Drinking from the wine-cellars they came across, they quickly added rape and murder to grand theft. If anyone had held out hope that the Eastern and Western church might eventually heal the great schism, the fourth Crusade effectively widened the split past the point of no return. Yet a total of eight principal crusades were conducted in all.

The Spiritual Decline of the Church

Sadly, some of the leaders of the church during much of the Middle Ages didn't behave much better. Spiritual integrity pretty much bottomed out around the 11th century. As the Eastern and Western centers of the church remained at odds with one another, one choice of pope might be rejected by the other section of the church, which would choose its own. (Occasionally there were three popes in power at the same time.) Due to the external pressures on the church, popes and other church leaders were sometimes chosen more because of political clout, personal favor, administrative skills, a hefty bribe, or numerous other reasons that had little to do with spiritual qualifications.

Hundreds of church offices and titles were created for the sole purpose of selling them to interested parties (a practice known as *simony*). And it was during this time that the church began the selling of *indulgences*, which was later challenged and eliminated along with simony. As the Middle Ages came to a close, the church was working toward a phase of spiritual renewal.

The Inquisition (1200 and onward)

What Communism was to Congress in the 1950s and witchcraft was to Salem in the 1690s, *heresy* was to the medieval church. As the church attempted to purge itself of heresy, things got a bit out of

QUESTIONS?

What was the deal with indulgences?

The concept of indulgences was based on the thinking that certain Christians died with good works to spare and breezed their way into heaven. And the church allowed other people to purchase those "extra" good works. The sale of indulgences turned out to be a phenomenal money maker for the church, and is said to have funded St. Peter's Cathedral among other grand projects. Big service projects such as fighting in the Crusades could also earn indulgences. One seller of indulgences at the time even had a marketing slogan: "As the coin into the coffer rings, the soul from purgatory springs!"

SEE FOR YOURSELF

"But there were also false prophets in Israel, just as there will be false teachers among you. They will cleverly teach their destructive heresies about God and even turn against their Master who bought them. Theirs will be a swift and terrible end" (2 Peter 2:1).

Opposing heresy is a biblical mandate, although many inquisitors didn't leave it to God to see that those accused reached a "swift and terrible end."

SAYS WHO?

"If forgers and malefactors are put to death by the secular power, there is much more reason for excommunicating and even putting to death one convicted of heresy."—*St. Thomas Aquinas*

hand with the formation of "the Inquisition"—not a commission, but rather a series of inquiries.

Convictions were advantageous to the prosecutors, because the land of anyone found to be a heretic could be confiscated by those who arrested him. At times, torture was used by inquisitors to prompt "confessions." In one instance, both heretics and Christians were seeking sanctuary, and a church representative ordered: "Kill them all, for God will know his own."

Late in the 1400s, Ferdinand and Isabella sanctioned the Spanish Inquisition, which was largely responsible for the elimination of any Muslim influences taking root in Spain, Sicily, and other places. Jewish peoples were also among the victims of persecution due to the Inquisition.

Bubonic Plague (1347 and onward)

Another reason for the darkness of the era was the outbreak of the "black death," more accurately known as the bubonic plague. The nasty little disease (carried to humans from rats via fleas) made its debut in 1347 and lasted off and on for centuries thereafter. At one point the death rate of those infected was 90 percent but later fell to a "mere" 30 percent. The disease attacked the lymph nodes, making them discolored and foul-smelling. Children carried flower petals in their pockets in a desperate attempt to mask the stench. And in a society rife with both superstition and religious fervor, many people attributed their dire circumstances to the wrath of God.

Got a Light?

We could go into greater detail about some of the gloom and doom of the spiritual state of things during the Middle Ages. But instead let's turn on the light and take a look at some of the brighter spots.

The Orthodox Church Forms in Russia

As the Islamic armies stopped or slowed the migration of Christianity to the East, the resulting northward surge of evangelism turned out to be a good thing for lots of people. The conversion of Russian Prince Vladimir at around the turn of the first millennium opened the door to Christianity in Russia. The Russians imported priests, art, icons, and other church supplies from Constantinople rather than Rome. Theirs was an Orthodox practice of faith, which had a number of distinctives.

Orthodoxy (or "correct teaching") was more resistant to change when it came to religious matters. Its adherents went back to early church fathers for basic teachings. Orthodox believers placed much faith in the church councils that had met throughout the centuries (Nicaea, Chalcedon, and others), and considered their findings a "done deal" in regard to Christian doctrine.

Orthodox believers were big on ritual and placed great emphasis on the practice of the sacraments. Another distinctive was their acceptance of icons. The use of religious images (paintings, statues, and other symbols) to enhance one's religious experience is viewed as dangerous by some Christians in that it can border on idolatry. The Orthodox view, however, is that such images work as catalysts for deep and meaningful spiritual emotions and experiences.

The Rise of Monasteries

Perhaps the biggest religious success story during the Middle Ages was the ongoing development of monasteries. Christianity continued to spread, and many pagan tribes converted—sometimes all at once at the command of a newly converted leader. The church found itself unable to adequately train the large numbers of new believers. A three-year course of study formerly prepared new converts in what they were supposed to believe. Before long, however, the preparation time had dwindled to the 40-day period of Lent each year. (But lest we tend to think *they* were starting to slide, let's remember we're working our way through a *No-Brainer's Guide* on the same topic!)

The influx of new believers quickly "brought down the curve" of education and spiritual acumen within the church. As a result, certain dissatisfied church members began to drift away to pursue deeper truths through solitary meditation and soul-searching. Eventually, some of these deep-thinking loners started bumping into each other out in the wilderness and decided to get together and form monasteries.

TRIVIA TIDBIT

The next time you sing "Ring Around the Rosie" with your kids, be aware that you're commemorating the deaths of those who fell victim to the Black Death. The "all fall down" part wasn't nearly so much fun during the Middle Ages.

TRIVIA TIDBIT

Augustine was also a writer whose works were well known among church people. His *Confessions* was a groundbreaking, personally revealing autobiography. *City of God* provided insight on how history and religion were somewhat interrelated. Both of these works, as well as his other writings, have continued to influence people throughout the centuries.

Augustine had been among the first to get things started in the fourth century. After a life of higher education and a thirst for truth, he had become a Christian. As an intellectual *and* a believer, he was able to combine philosophy with theology without weakening either.

More Fun than a Barrel of Monks?

Monastery involvement took on a new passion during the Middle Ages. In fact, the monks were known to some as "athletes of God." And in later years, those in the Franciscan order were so perky and filled with joy that they were called "jesters of God." Here are just a few of the leaders who were involved to some degree with the monastic movement during the thousand years of the Middle Ages:

Benedict (approximately 480–550)

Asceticism had been getting out of control with people flogging themselves, chaining themselves in caves, spending much of their lives alone atop poles, and performing other fanatical feats. Benedict sought better balance between Bible knowledge and practice. He exhorted people who wanted to pursue a godly lifestyle to work, study, eat, sleep, and help those who were needy. He is known for his 80-page "Rule" (a la *Roberts' Rules of Order*) which was essentially a *No-Brainer's Guide to Running a Good Monastery.* Many later monastic groups used Benedict's Rule as an invaluable handbook.

Gregory (approximately 540–604)

Perhaps you've heard of Gregorian chants, so named because Gregory strongly promoted music in church. But he was known just as much for his preaching and his missionary outreach. He was well respected as a writer, reformer, and eventually, pope.

The Venerable Bede (approximately 673–735)

A monk who wrote the first history of the English church, Bede was also influential among his peers for his commentaries on Old Testament Scripture. His discription of seventh-century England shows little difference between pagan and church leaders, both of them being tribal leaders who succeeded or failed based on their ability to win bloody military victories on the battlefields.

Boniface (680–754)

After living as a monk in England until age 40, Boniface is perhaps best known as a missionary who traveled to France, Germany, and the low countries of Europe. In Germany he founded a Benedictine monastery that continued to focus on missions for a long while.

Bernard of Clairvaux (1090–1153)

Abbot of the Cistercian Abbey of Clairvaux, Bernard is credited with "O Sacred Head, Now Wounded" and other hymns of the church. He has also been called the most important preacher of the Middle Ages. Bernard influenced popes as well as common people by expanding their understanding of who Jesus was. He challenged them to see Jesus as a tender and compassionate figure rather than solely as a severe judge.

Francis of Assisi (1182–1226)

In response to a vision while a young man, Francis created the *friars* ("brothers") who professed allegiance to church authority while focusing their efforts on helping laypeople. Francis and his followers renounced family ties and personal possessions. He is often remembered as "the most perfect Christian since Christ."

Thomas Aquinas (approximately 1225–1274)

Nominations for the "Christian Man of the 13th Century" usually weigh heavily in favor of Thomas Aquinas. As people of his time began to rediscover the writings and importance of Aristotle, Thomas began to apply those basic philosophies to Christianity. He emphasized the importance of logic and reason in regard to faith, while allowing that no matter how much we might discover in such pursuits, God remains a mystery. While he was at it, he gathered all the information available at the time in numerous areas of the arts and sciences, and created a systematic method to show how it all integrated with Christian faith.

SAYS WHO?

"He who comes not willingly to church shall one day go unwillingly to hell."
—*The Venerable Bede*

TRIVIA TIDBIT

Francis of Assisi was known to experience the ongoing appearance of *stigmata* (bleeding wounds in the places Jesus had been pierced—hands, feet, side, and brow). This phenomenon occurred so frequently that it is thought that the regular oozing of blood might have hastened his death.

QUESTIONS?

Where were the women leaders during this era of church history?

As the monasteries proved a worthwhile pursuit for men during the Middle Ages, several separate women's groups formed as well. The women didn't tend to travel and teach, yet a few rose to prominence due to their writing. Some memorable works include the mystical, musical, and scientific writings of Hildegard of Bingen, the call to papal reform of Catherine of Siena, and the poetry of Hadewijch. While not exactly household names, these women (and others) were active for God.

The Few . . . the Not-So-Proud

So even though the church might have been suffering from a number of problems during the Middle Ages, a regular stream of good men and women went into the monasteries to pursue a more intimate knowledge of God. As they did, their influence became more than merely theological. For example, since many of the monasteries were self-sufficient, the monks had learned the finer aspects of farming, tending to livestock, and other practical skills. Their expertise led to natural conversations with local farmers, which frequently would lead to spiritual matters as well.

And even though the initial concept of monasteries was to get away from the "crowds" in the church for more personal introspection, many of the monks had an effective evangelistic outreach into communities that might never have much contact with the established church. Indeed, during the Middle Ages, all the average person on the street (or more likely, the dirt road) knew about the church was what he or she learned from a parish priest. Not surprisingly, rivalries between the monks of the monastery and the local priests were not uncommon.

Other Events of the Middle Ages

Here are a few other significant church events of the Middle Ages:

- 1065—Westminster Abbey was consecrated.
- 1170—Thomas à Becket was murdered. In an extreme case of church vs. state authority, Thomas (Archbishop of Canterbury) was assassinated by knights from the court of England's King Henry II, who had once been a close friend.
- 1384—John Wyclif(fe) died after having initiated an English version of the Latin Bible. He was labeled a heretic and condemned by the Pope. He managed to die a natural death, but the church dug him up in 1427 and burned his bones.
- 1415—John Hus(s) was martyred. Wycliffe's teachings had inspired religious revival in Bohemia (now the Czech Republic), where popular preacher John Hus spoke boldly of the authority

of Scripture over that of the church. After promising him immunity so they could talk to him, the church labeled him a heretic, broke their promise, and burned him at the stake.

- 1418—*Imitation of Christ* was published. Thomas à Kempis, an Augustinian monk, wrote what is still considered a classic piece of devotional literature. The book was a call to self-discipline and a greater focus on Jesus for a more satisfying spiritual life.

Yet in spite of the schisms, arguments, politics, wars, diseases, and other divisive elements of the Middle Ages, the church endured. Other than the exodus of devoted people from churches into monasteries, we have seen only one "split," as such, between East and West. However, a primary fault line had formed between those who endorsed church business as usual and those who were determined to see changes made.

As the European civilized world stood on the brink of a Renaissance and Age of Enlightenment, the church was ready for one as well. And as a result, the church would be split for good—further complicating a precise definition of "what Christians believe."

Questions to Ponder and/or Discuss

1. Determine where you would place yourself on each of the following scales.

When it comes to people who don't believe as I do, I am:

_____

Completely tolerant   Insistent they conform

I would find more satisfaction if involved in:

_____

An isolated, monastic lifestyle   A crowded church

My evangelistic methods are more like:

_____

A pleading child   The Spanish Inquisition

When I disagree with church policy, I tend to:

_____

Stay and try to effect change   Split

2. A thousand years from now, what do you think historians will record as the biggest problem(s) with the church of this era? What do you predict will be the positive things they have to say?

3. Who are the people who seem to have the biggest influence on your religious understanding? (They may be either noted authors/speakers or local people you know.) List all you can think of.

CHAPTER ELEVEN

"WATCHING HOW FAST THESE GUYS SPLIT, YOU'D THINK I WAS LOOKING AT THE CHURCH."

Let's Make Like the Church and Split

CHURCH HISTORY FROM A.D. 1500 UNTIL TODAY

These days if you want to protest something, you have a lot of options. You might write your congressperson. If that doesn't work, you can run for office yourself and work the system to right any wrongs you find. You can start petitions throughout your neighborhood. You can boycott. You can picket. You can write protest songs. You can pen an angry letter to the editor of the newspaper. In today's culture, there are many ways to be heard, even if you're in the minority.

Yet any time you attempt to stand against a force much larger and more powerful than yourself, your voice tends to be lost among the cacophony produced by the greater force. People who persevere against such great odds tend to get noticed, as is witnessed in the success of such movies as *All the President's Men* or *Erin Brockovich*.

In 16th-century Europe, perhaps no force was as great as the church. Sure, it had faced some obstacles and divisions, as we have seen. Yet it was still the big dog on the block. Even the monarchies

SOME THINGS YOU'LL DISCOVER IN THIS CHAPTER

1. How Protestantism got started

2. Why we have so many Protestant denominations

3. Renewal within the Catholic Church, parallel to the Reformation

SAYS WHO?

"The dissenter is every human being at those moments of his life when he resigns momentarily from the herd and thinks for himself."—*Archibald MacLeish*

SEE FOR YOURSELF

Here are a couple of passages that made a big difference in Martin Luther's life. (Of course, his version was in Latin.)

"For in the gospel a righteousness from God is revealed, a righteousness that is by faith from first to last, just as it is written, 'The righteous will live by faith' " (Romans 1:17, NIV).

"But now God has shown us a different way of being right in his sight—not by obeying the law but by the way promised in the Scriptures long ago. We are made right in God's sight when we trust in Jesus Christ to take away our sins. And we can all be saved in this same way, no matter who we are or what we have done" (Romans 3:21-22).

120

and kingdoms of the time, as powerful as they were, were localized. The church spanned all of them. And from the crowning of Charlemagne (800) onward, church leaders had frequently rivaled national leaders in terms of ultimate power and prestige.

As we saw in the last chapter, speaking against the church could quickly lead to charges of heresy, ending in excommunication, inquisition, or worse. And for many people it was simply easier to go along with what the church said whether or not you agreed.

Move over Dr. Atkins, It's the Diet of Worms

But it seems that certain people are never able to keep their mouths shut when confronted with situations they don't agree with. One such person in the early 1500s was Martin Luther, a German in his thirties who had been a monk almost half his life. Luther studied Scripture and was known for six-hour confessions, yet he had never been able to feel at peace with God. When his mentors had no other answers for him, one suggested Luther pursue a doctoral degree in religious studies. (If nothing else, the work should keep him busy.)

It was from this academic pursuit that Luther struggled with biblical statements about righteousness that finally put things in perspective for him. He began to comprehend what he called *passive righteousness.*

Luther had done everything within his power to be a decent monk and a good Christian. Yet no matter how hard he tried, he never felt free of the weight of sin in his life. However, he finally came to the clear realization that, "The righteous shall live by faith." In response, he said, "Now I felt as though I had been reborn altogether and had entered Paradise."

As soon as Luther began to crystallize his beliefs that salvation and righteousness had more to do with faith than with good works, he began to stand out in a church that at the time was still peddling indulgences. So while many were buying tickets to heaven, Luther began to spread the word that he had found a free entrance.

But how now could this lone voice stand against a power as great as the church? He started in 1517 with his well-publicized act of nailing his "95 Theses" on the door of the Wittenberg cathedral. The action itself wasn't a defiance of the church, because the church door was the closest thing to the Internet of its time, where people would gather for news and interaction.

But *what* he hammered onto the door was essentially a Top 95 List of why indulgences weren't such a good or biblical idea. And in the next few years Luther had churned out a series of books that not only explained his personal views but also challenged the authority of the church. He was among the first to make good use of a recent invention: the printing press. Soon more than 300,000 of his books and pamphlets were in circulation. And by 1521 he had been summoned to appear at a hearing in Worms, Germany, before a diet (an official assembly) chaired by none other than Charles V, ruling both as the king of Spain and Germany's Holy Roman Emperor.

As Luther entered the room, he saw his works spread out over a table. When asked to officially recant what he had written, he replied, "Unless I am convinced by the testimony of the Scriptures or by clear reason (for I do not trust either in the pope or in councils alone, since it is well known that they have often erred and contradicted themselves), I am bound by the Scriptures. I have quoted and my conscience is captive to the Word of God. I cannot and I will not retract anything, since it is neither safe nor honest to violate one's conscience."

And whoop, there it was. Luther held to his revolutionary belief in *sola fides*, *sola gratia*, and *sola scriptura* (faith alone, grace alone, and Scripture alone). It was possible for people to find their way to God and righteousness through faith rather than good works, and through the truths of Scripture without making concessions to the church. Rejected by both the pope and the emperor, Luther the protester spearheaded the entire Protestant movement. Yet his passion was not sparked from an outsider's antagonistic view of the church, but rather because he was one of its own and could not sanction all the customs and abuses he had witnessed firsthand.

Luther broke from the church rules in a big way. He got married,

TRIVIA TIDBIT

Between 1450 and 1500 the printing press made available more books than had been produced the 1,000 years previously. And compared to paying a scribe several month's wages for each book hand-copied, the books off the press were remarkably affordable as well.

TRIVIA TIDBIT

The seven sacraments of the church were: (1) Baptism, administered at birth; (2) Confirmation, when a child began to reason for himself or herself; (3) Penance, in response to sins; (4) Communion; (5) Marriage; (6) Ordination, for those committing themselves to the church, and (7) Extreme unction, also known as last rites, administered to those about to die. Luther's concern was that the church overemphasized such things to the point that they became potential sources of pride and/or self-righteousness, so Lutherans retained only baptism and communion as sacraments.

QUESTIONS?

For whom is Tyndale House Publishers, responsible for the No-Brainer's Series and other fine products, named for?

William Tyndale (1490?–1536) was a contemporary of Martin Luther who developed a passion to provide a copy of the Scriptures in English—a novel idea for his time. Tyndale's translation of the New Testament was soundly rejected by the established church, but bootleg copies were soon being circulated. Tyndale started work on the Old Testament, but the church put an end to his work by putting an end to him. He was executed in 1536, but others completed the entire Bible in English. Tyndale's version was used as a reference for the King James Bible, published in 1611.

rejected five of the seven church sacraments, challenged churches to give up many of their holdings (up to 30 percent of the available land in many parts of Germany), rejected the hierarchy of priests within the church, and even went so far as to label the Pope "Antichrist" because Luther felt the church did more to occlude people's understanding of the Gospel than to promote it.

You might think that with Luther's bold stand, the church world would soon be divided into two large forces: Catholic vs. Protestant. It was, but only for a short time. If we visualize the church as a great timber log, we know that due to the great schism and other internal struggles, the log already had a few cracks and chinks in it. Luther's nail into the door of the Wittenberg Cathedral was like a wedge being driven into the trunk, and the resulting Protestant movement followed up with such force that the great log, which had remained in one piece for almost sixteen centuries, was suddenly two.

Now we're about to see, however, that while the Catholic ("universal") church remained essentially united, the Protestant portion will continue to divide and subdivide into considerably smaller pieces of kindling.

One Church, Two Church, Old Church, New Church

From this point onward, we'll attempt to step up our progress through church history. If you wish to know more about any particular denomination or event, many good resources are available to help you delve deeper.

The Lutherans

Martin Luther had quite a following from others who were alarmed at what they were seeing take place within the church, so the Lutherans flourished. But in spite of Luther's opposition to various church tenets, he pretty much held to their belief that at communion (the Eucharist) the bread and wine somehow literally became the body and blood of Christ—a concept known as *transubstantiation*.

A Swiss peer of Luther's, Ulrich Zwingli, went along with essen-

tially all of Luther's reform proposals, but he could not endorse transubstantiation from a scientific point of view. So Zwingli's followers branched off from the Lutherans and soon divided again into two major groups.

The Calvinists

Some of Zwingli's followers joined forces with those of John Calvin, a rising Protestant leader who helped popularize the sermon as a method of explaining Scripture. Calvin is known for his belief in predestination—that all humans are sinful and deserving of hell but that God before the world began chose certain ones to be saved. Calvin also maintained a strong work ethic. Essentially any job was "godly" if God was given the glory for it, so Calvinists became noted for their dedication and hard work. Calvin was probably the leading figure of the Protestant Reformation after Luther.

Calvinists also designed an organized structure that appealed to many people. Local churches, led by elders and deacons, were grouped into regions and sent representatives to interact on a regular basis. The regional groups, in turn, sent representatives to national gatherings. This structure was (and is) called *presbyterian* government.

The Anabaptists

Other followers of Zwingli desired even more changes than either he or Luther had made in church practice. They wanted a clean break of the close connection that church and state had held since Constantine. Rather than being considered "Christian" because you happened to be born in a nation with a Christian leader, they perceived Christians to be those who actively pursued a life of faith and devotion to God. Consequently, they rejected the practice of baptizing infants, and decided that baptism should accompany a person's decision to follow Christ as an adult. Their theology was heavily based on certain teachings of Christ, such as the Sermon on the Mount. They refused to swear oaths, spoke against capital punishment, and many formed communal churches based on the first-century church.

These groups were quickly labeled Anabaptists ("rebaptizers")

TRIVIA TIDBIT

A renowned Calvinist/Presbyterian in Scotland was named John Knox. He made much headway for Protestants into the predominantly Catholic domain of Mary, Queen of Scots.

SEE FOR YOURSELF

Jesus' Sermon on the Mount is found in Matthew 5–7. And indeed, He challenges His listeners to pursue standards that are quite different from the rest of the world. The Anabaptists were one group who interpreted this portion of Scripture more literally than others.

QUESTIONS?

Why was opposition so strong against a group who was only trying to follow biblical mandates?

The Anabaptist practice of re-baptizing smacked of spiritual arrogance to onlookers, even if it was genuine and heartfelt. Their refusal to take oaths became equated with anarchy in some cases. But then one group of German Anabaptists armed themselves, took over a city, and declared themselves "the new Israel" preparing the way for Jesus.

Even though such behavior was definitely atypical of Anabaptist beliefs, and the rebels were soon defeated, the incident fueled opposition toward the sect and validated suspicions that the group had dangerous potential.

and were scorned and persecuted, even by other Protestant groups. Because swearing oaths was traditionally involved in business deals, in courtrooms, in expressing loyalty to a nation, etc., belonging to this sect became grounds for execution in some countries. A favorite method of sentencing the offenders was drowning.

One Dutch Anabaptist leader was named Menno Simons, from whom the Mennonites took their name.

The Anglicans

While some Protestant denominations were springing up in opposition to state connections, another was being formed for the express purpose of becoming a state church. Because of his desperate desire for a male heir, King Henry VIII wanted to dump wife number one (Catherine of Aragon) in order to marry his mistress, Anne Boleyn, who was pregnant. But his request for a marriage annulment was rejected by Pope Clement.

Rather than submit to the authority of the church, Henry "fired" it. He simply declared that the Pope no longer had authority in England. A "Reformation Parliament" was soon called to ratify the split. The Archbishop of Canterbury, Thomas Cranmer (a Protestant), became the top religious figure in England and okayed Henry's divorce.

Soon the Act of Supremacy was passed, which placed the English king above any religious authority in the new Church of England, or Anglican Church. Church funds that once went to Rome now went instead to the royal treasury. Certain Catholic leaders in England who opposed the change were executed (Sir Thomas More, for example). So were Protestant leaders who spoke too strongly about the need for additional reformation.

And for all of Henry's scheming, which resulted in a brand new Protestant denomination, his new bride failed to deliver him a male heir. Like so many others who disappointed Henry, Anne Boleyn lost her head, quite literally.

The Puritans

England became strongly Protestant during the reign of Henry VIII and his successor, Edward VI. But Edward was followed by Mary I, the "Bloody Mary" of history, who was a devout Catholic. Several prominent Protestants were killed during her reign. Others hid or fled. Mary was followed by Elizabeth I who declared herself Protestant, and many of the exiles returned to England.

Some of the Protestants who continued to argue for greater reform throughout this period belonged to a Calvinist group called the Puritans, but Puritanism always remained a minority belief. They resisted the close ties between the church and government in England, and they emphasized preaching over adherence to the book of Common Prayer.

Some Puritans continued to attempt reform within the Church of England. Others separated under the name of Congregationalists and were among the first to sail to the colonies for the opportunity to worship as they wished. Some Congregationalists, influenced by the Mennonites, became the General Baptists in England.

The Jesuits

For a number of years, conflicts over religion got quite messy. Many of the wars fought in England and Europe had numerous causes, but religion usually came into play at some level. Many people were killed apart from out-and-out warfare because persecution and rivalries were quite common.

And it wasn't simply a matter of the Protestants seeking changes while the Catholics sat around and did nothing. Indeed, many people within the Catholic Church were working hard for reform. And for decades, many of the Protestant groups were looking to work *with* the Catholic Church rather than against it in seeking mutually acceptable doctrines and church practices.

The Jesuits were a group of fervent believers who devoted themselves to reform within the church. Preceded by other well-respected religious orders active in the early 1500s, the Jesuits were founded in 1534 by Ignatius Loyola and soon became some of the most dynamic Christians in the history of England. Their personal discipleship training, based on Loyola's work titled *Spiritual Exercises*, soon made them much in demand as teachers and missionaries. Loyola's spiritual zeal has been compared to Martin Luther's.

When it came to early missions beyond Europe, the Catholics far

TRIVIA TIDBIT

In the years when Columbus was first poking around in the New World, Thomas More was learning law and logic. After developing a sterling reputation, he became Chancellor of England from 1529 to 1532. But he could not endorse Henry VIII's political, religious, and personal shenanigans. His loyalty was questioned and he was eventually put on trial, found guilty of being a traitor, and beheaded in 1535. More's story is told in the classic play *A Man for All Seasons*. He was made a saint by the Catholic Church in 1935.

QUESTIONS?

What was the significance of the Book of Common Prayer?

The *Book of Common Prayer,* issued in 1549 under Thomas Cranmer, was the official liturgy of the Church of England. Revised several times until 1662, it simplified the old medieval Latin service books into a single volume, in English, that was used by both priests and church members. The Anglican Church still uses prayer books based on this centuries-old work.

TRIVIA TIDBIT

One early Catholic missionary was Francis Xavier, a follower of Ignatius Loyola who has been compared to Paul in his enthusiasm to take the Gospel to new parts of the world. He spent years in India and later served in Ceylon, Indonesia, and Japan. He died awaiting the opportunity to go into China.

SAYS WHO?

"I look upon all the world as my parish." —*John Wesley*

outshone the Protestants. The Jesuits and other orders soon established numerous Christian outposts in Africa, Asia, and "the new world."

The Methodists

Fast forward a century or so to the mid-1700s and two brothers, John and Charles Wesley. They were adherents of Luther's teaching that salvation comes by grace through faith, and they took to the streets to spread the word. John Wesley was a prominent preacher, often speaking outdoors to whomever would listen. Charles worked with him but is usually remembered more for his skill as a hymn writer.

One of the Wesleys' theological distinctives was the belief that God's grace restored free will to people and that believers could lose their salvation if they chose a course of ongoing sin without repentance. In contrast, however, believers who devoted themselves to their faith could accomplish "Christian perfection"—not sinlessness, but a point where every conscious thought and action was to the glory of God. They were eventually called Methodists because of their method of organization: believers were clustered into small-group cells for ongoing Bible study and spiritual growth. The new group was also involved in active social work, being formed in the shadow of the Industrial Revolution.

That Will Be the Deism

This was an exciting and challenging time for believers. Those within the church were being freed to choose a number of options in regard to matters of doctrine and how to practice their faith. But outside the church, society as a whole was beginning to question the necessity of having any religion at all.

It was the Age of Enlightenment, and things would never be the same in science *or* religion. The tendency of the ancient Greek and Roman scholars had been to observe and ponder, but the intellectuals of the sixteenth century were discovering the value of scientific theory to *predict* what would happen.

A case in point was Isaac Newton's discovery of the law of gravity that explained everything from apples falling from trees to planets spinning through the universe. This single law of nature crystallized thinking in regard to a lot of matters, and allowed others to build on Newton's findings and go on to new and more enlightening discoveries.

No longer were people content with accepting much on faith. Scientific thinkers wanted to "prove" the existence of God. The authority of Scripture, the driving force of the church for centuries, was no longer good enough for them. Many assumed there had to be a religious equivalent to the law of gravity—a way of thinking that would explain and simplify God to everyone's satisfaction.

To their credit, many of these people had grown weary of bloody wars being fought in the name of religion. In addition, their prior assumptions that Christian morality must be the cornerstone of any civilized society had been shattered. Explorers had returned with tales of China and various faraway lands, describing people of other religions who were as socially attuned as the Europeans, if not more so.

As a result, a new belief system was formed called *deism*. In attempting to combine the essence of all known religions into a religious unified theory, many of the distinctives of Christianity had to go. The virgin birth couldn't be explained by science or reason. Gone! The accounts of all the miracles? Outta here! The resurrection of Jesus? Buh-bye.

Eventually the best explanation deists could provide for God was that He may have created the world but apparently relinquished control and abandoned it. With this definition of "religion," many of the great thinkers could still claim to be religious. But their version was a far cry from the Christianity of the previous centuries. It was around that time that many people began to reject the teaching that the Bible was divinely inspired. And deistic thinking continues to influence many intellectuals who still want to consider the possibility of a higher power without getting personal about it.

SAYS WHO?

"Religion is an illusion and it derives its strength from the fact that it falls in with our instinctual desires."
—*Sigmund Freud*

"We have just enough religion to make us hate, but not enough to make us love one another."—*Jonathan Swift*

The Value of Pietism

In contrast to the deists, another group formed who were known as the *pietists*. Like the deists, many in this group bemoaned the current state of Christian religion. They too hated the wars between Protestants and Catholics, and were saddened by the dull, dry practice of religion in many churches of the time.

But the pietists had a different solution. Rather than attempting to rationalize and secularize faith, they attempted to make it more personal and intimate. They weren't convinced the Reformation of the church was yet complete, and their desire was to go beyond getting the doctrines correct and begin to actually practice what they preached. At the time, this type of thinking was just as revolutionary as the deists' attempts to elevate reason above faith.

Pietist groups sprang up in England, on the European continent, and even in the newly forming colonies in America. Theology and lifestyle combined for these groups, which were typified by individual and group prayers, Bible study, devotions, and service to others.

By the end of the 18th century, the trend had expanded into a renewed passion and emotional outflow that was getting lost in the wake of the Age of Enlightenment. This was known as *Romanticism* and was not primarily a religious movement. Yet many writers and artists, fed up with so many scientific and industrial advances, started recalling "the good old days" of the past. Novels became prominent in literature, many looking backward, such as Sir Walter Scott's *Ivanhoe*. Other Romantic artists include Beethoven, Wagner, Lord Byron, Shelley, Wordsworth, Coleridge, and others.

And Denomination Goes to . . .

As you can see, the church has come a long way from its simple beginning, when everyone met together and all were of the same heart and mind. The developments we've seen in the past few chapters were only a beginning, yet a trend had been set. Many of today's denominations and independent churches were formed during later generations as various segments pulled away from one

group to merge with another or start their own worship practice. Sometimes a denomination rolls along, strong and vital for decades, but eventually it becomes too liberal or too conservative for a number of its members. If the dissatisfied members can't change the denomination, they'll jump spiritual ships or start a new offshoot of their own.

During the past century we have witnessed powerful movements toward liberal Christianity, a pendulum swing in the opposite direction to fundamentalism, a more middle-of-the-road rise of evangelicalism, a strong emphasis on Charismatic renewal, a noteworthy Vatican council to regroup and re-ignite the passion of Catholic believers, and more.

The growth of Christianity has been more successful in recent years in places other than Europe and the United States. Currently both Africa and Asia have more Christians than North America, and Latin America has the highest *percentage* of people who define themselves as Christians—93 percent.

Christian churches comprised primarily of African-Americans have also done quite well during the past century—and it's about time. Even in the early development of European-sponsored missions in North America, some imported African slaves when the missionaries didn't want to impose harsh work demands on the natives. Later, during the Civil War, both slavery and anti-slavery groups used the Bible to support their views. And if someone cared enough to evangelize a slave, he would usually emphasize the "thou shalt not steal" and submission passages of Scripture.

Every once in a while, organizations are formed that attempt to pull believers of various denominations together, with varying success. While the unity of believers is a worthy goal, attempts at unification frequently result in many participants feeling they must sacrifice too much of what they have come to believe.

So after all these chapters taking us down the Memory Lane of church history, perhaps you can see the potential problems in presenting a clear-cut explanation of "what Christians believe." Name a topic, and you're likely to find good Christians who will take two or more opposing viewpoints. The best a book like this can do is try

TRIVIA TIDBIT

A teenage slave named Richard Allen exemplified such a change in lifestyle after his conversion that his master also became a Christian. In time the master freed Richard, who went on to establish the Negro Episcopal Church, which eventually became the African Methodist Episcopal (A.M.E.) Church (1816). Today, about a third of the approximately 13 million Methodists in the United States are African-American, and other denominations have significant African-American populations as well.

to hit the high points, shoot for the majority agreement, and remind you of your right to agree or disagree.

Perhaps one of the better advancements of recent theological thought is agreeing to disagree. Some places still continue to literally battle over religious beliefs, and even believers in more tolerant locations may not be immune from persecution if they practice a minority faith amid larger, more accepted ones. Yet in a few geographic regions, diverse religions are learning to coexist, even though it is an ongoing struggle to maintain mutual respect.

For decades, the Hatfield and McCoy families made a name for themselves by maintaining a famous feud. The story (which some dispute) goes that the feuding began in 1863 and escalated in 1878 when one family stole a pig from the other. The feud ran for 30 years and left an estimated 20 family members dead. The Hatfields and McCoys were perhaps the biggest rivals since the Montagues and Capulets. The name alone was enough to spark violence.

The same can be true of denominations within the church. Perhaps we make too much of our religious monikers. If one person calls himself a Baptist and another calls herself a Catholic, that's enough for some people to start taking potshots. Yet what do those denominational labels really say about the totality of the person? Mother Teresa devoted her life to God and did what she felt called to do. So did Billy Graham. Isn't there room in the world for both examples—and for anyone else who wishes to pursue a life of righteousness and respond to the promptings of God in his or her life?

Perhaps there's hope. In 2000, the Hatfields and McCoys made the news in another way: the two families got together for a picnic. The biggest feuding that day took place on the softball field and during a tug-of-war. And lo and behold, they had so much fun they scheduled future get-togethers.

Sometimes the *relationship* between people needs to take prominence over any labels or titles. If we want to speak up when someone offends us personally and directly, that's a natural response. But if we find ourselves rejecting others simply because of a different church affiliation, perhaps it's time to drop the crusader's sword and extend a piece of fried chicken instead.

Questions to Ponder and/or Discuss

1. If you are Protestant, what are your feelings about the religion of the Catholics? If Catholic, how do you feel about the Protestants? How much do you know personally about the other's doctrines, and how much consists of second- or third-hand information you've heard from other people?

2. What do you know about the history of your own denomination? If your knowledge is vague, do a little research into your spiritual roots.

3. What do you know about the lives of more recent religious figures? Below is a list of people you might want to use as subjects for short biographical research to fill any gaps remaining in your quest of noteworthy Christians and what they believe.

Jonathan Edwards (1703–1758)

William Penn (1644–1718)

William Booth (1829–1912) and Evangeline Cory Booth (1865–1950)

James Hudson Taylor (1832–1905)

Watchman Nee (1903–1972)

Reinhold Niebuhr (1892–1971)

Billy Sunday (1862–1935)

C. S. Lewis (1898–1963)

Martin Luther King, Jr. (1929–1968)

Phoebe Palmer (1807–1874)

George Whitefield (1714–1770)

David Livingstone (1813–1873)

Karl Barth (1886–1968)

Dietrich Bonhoeffer (1906–1945)

Mother Teresa (1910–1997)

D. L. Moody (1837–1899)

Billy Graham (1918–)

Admittedly, with a few exceptions this list is predominantly American, Caucasian, and Protestant. And it barely begins to cover the key figures of the time periods represented. But feel free to add any other figures from your own history/ ethnic group/ denomination and see what you can discover.

PART THREE

Where the Church Meets the Culture

"ONE FOR ME, ONE FOR YOU, ONE FOR THE CHURCH, ONE FOR ME, ONE FOR YOU, ONE FOR THE CHURCH . . ."

CHAPTER TWELVE

Behavior Self

MORALITY AND VALUES

So far in this book we've tried to see "what Christians believe" from a *doctrinal* point of view. We've also taken a *historical* view to demonstrate why Christians don't necessarily believe the same thing on any given topic. And yet we suspect you might be looking for more.

In everyday conversations when the topic arises of "what Christians believe," people may occasionally want to know "Who is God?" or "What do you think about angels?" or "Why do you guys drink those little cups of juice?" So a working knowledge of doctrine and church practice is important.

Yet more frequently we tend to get pointed questions about delicate topics such as abortion, homosexuality, a woman's place in the world, capital punishment, and so forth. In many cases our peers have heard a prominent, outspoken Christian take a hard line on one of these topics, and they want to know if *all* Christians feel the same way.

Perhaps nowhere are Christians more divided than when it comes to some of these issues. While we have come to a basic agreement on most of the key doctrines, we vary in our opinions of how far to

SAYS WHO?

"We have, in fact, two kinds of morality side by side; one which we preach but do not practice, and another which we practice but seldom preach."
—*Bertrand Russell*

SAYS WHO?

"Conviction without experience makes for harshness."—*Flannery O'Connor*

extend our displays of grace, mercy, forgiveness, and such. How much is enough? Can you take these qualities too far?

In our historical rearview mirror, we see similar problems in the past that weren't always handled so well. Is our desire to promote the cause of Christ to people who haven't heard? Good idea! But send a hoard of hostile knights and peasants to beat some religious sensitivity into our opponents? Another series of Crusades might not be the best approach. Keep heresy out of the church? A noble goal. But starting another inquisition with the use of torture to gain "confessions" would surely become another black mark in church history.

So as we turn our attention to some of the topics of the twenty-first century, we're likely to rouse a lot of strong opinions and powerful passions. While we may not come to many unifying answers, given the wide range of Christian beliefs, we at least want to raise some common questions that nonbelievers are asking. Sometimes it's not so much *what* we say in return, but *how* we say it that will cause them to decide whether or not to listen to us.

B.Y.O.B. (Bring Your Own Background)

In the closing chapters of this book we'll try to cover many of the "hot topics" facing Christians in society today. But first let's consider an even more basic concern. Some of our non-Christian friends who know we're believers might ask us: "If I become a Christian, will I have to give up drinking, smoking, playing the lottery, reading my daily horoscope, going to movies, dancing, listening to rock 'n' roll or country/western music, etc.?"

Few groups oppose *everything* on this list, and even fewer would say that involvement in these things will result in a divine cancellation notice regarding your salvation. Yet each item on the list is deemed offensive by certain Christian groups and/or churches that frown on such activities as secular threats to any Christian believer.

Even the most tolerant churches have to draw the line *somewhere*. A genuine conversion to Christianity necessitates changes in thoughts, speech, and behavior. Murderers can be forgiven and embraced by the love of the church, but in return they must stop whacking people who make them angry. Thieves can be redeemed and join the body of believers, but their future tithes shouldn't come from fencing the neighbors' stereo equipment.

Several decades ago, people would occasionally throw "Come As You Are" parties. In an era when it was customary to put on fancy clothes to attend informal parties (and even ball games!), it was a novel idea to throw a spur of the moment get-together that would allow people to show up in everyday clothes, coveralls, curlers, robe and pajamas, or whatever they happened to be wearing at the time.

The appeal of Christianity is that God extends a "come as you are" invitation to sinful humans. Jesus was never exclusive or picky about whom He spent time with. The woman at the well had been through five husbands, and was living with yet another man whom she wasn't married to. Jesus' extended conversation with her resulted in the conversion of many in her Samaritan village (John 4). He refused to condemn the woman who had been caught in the act of adultery (John 8:10-11). He readily forgave the repentant thief on the cross. He went to the home of Zacchaeus, a crooked tax collector. He embraced children and lepers—two groups of people who were frequently neglected. And following His example, the Christian church remains to this day a "come as you are" place to seek mercy, forgiveness, and acceptance.

Yet the church was never intended to be a "stay as you are" institution. Jesus demonstrated this point as well. Once He was approached by a wealthy young man who wanted to be a disciple. Jesus loved the guy. The guy loved Jesus. But when Jesus challenged him to make a change in his lifestyle, the man refused, and Jesus allowed him to walk away (Mark 10:17-22). Similarly, any genuine conversion to Christianity should result in changes for the better. We need to be willing to allow God to expose any sin in our lives, and then we need to eliminate those sins out of love for and obedience to Him.

This is trickier than it may seem. As good as we get at hiding the fact, many of us are not perfect. In fact, we may hide some of our

QUESTIONS?

How do Christians know when to stick with helping someone and when it's time to give up on him or her?

Each person's situation is different, so believers need to remain responsive to the leading of the Holy Spirit. If facing hard-headed and hard-hearted resistance from others, the best strategy might be to "shake off [the] dust from your feet as you leave" (Luke 9:5). Yet many times we discover that our God-provided qualities of patience and perseverance eventually pay off. Just because someone isn't immediately responsive to us doesn't mean we can't continue to show love to the person, pray for him or her, and keep looking for God's timing and/or the right opportunity to make a difference in the person's life.

TRIVIA TIDBIT

The practice of *excommunication*, or forced removal of someone from the church for disciplinary purposes, has been around for a long time. In biblical times, such a punishment would have had a serious social impact as well as a religious one, with the goal of having the person repent and return to fellowship with all his or her friends. As the church gained power during the Middle Ages, excommunication became a common means of discipline. At times, popes have used it against entire nations.

sins so well that *we* don't even see them. And even after we discover them tucked away in some deep dark crevice of the soul, it can take much effort and time to eliminate them.

We've come to see this in chemical addictions such as alcoholism or drug use. But experts tell us that other behaviors can be addictive as well—sexual activity, food intake, gambling, and so forth. So when the individual can't overcome his or her sins immediately upon conversion, which is frequently the case, the church is there for the person for the long run. Patience, mercy, and grace are extended to struggling souls who want to rid their lives of sins that have been around perhaps for decades.

On the other hand, what if someone tries to take advantage of a loving, caring, patient body of believers? This has been a problem since the formation of the church. In Paul's writings, he was horrified to discover that certain people had heard that God's grace was free and abundant and had responded by assuming, *Whoopee! Now we can sin all we want to and cash in on easy forgiveness* (Romans 6:1-4).

In an extreme example, one of the regular attendees in the early Corinthian church was boldly "living in sin with his father's wife"—a blatant disregard for both God's law and the acceptable social behavior for the time. Yet the church was "graciously" allowing it to take place (1 Corinthians 5:1-2). Paul didn't sigh or wink or suggest that the church should tolerate such a little scamp; he called for the expulsion of this man from the fellowship of the church until "his sinful nature will be destroyed" (v. 5).

Sometimes the church is placed in a quandary to determine when to be gracious and forgiving, and when to take more of a hard line if it senses certain members aren't really making much of an attempt to be Christ-like. Consequently, some contemporary churches may seem quite stern and rigid, while others have more of an "anything goes" tolerance. Groups at both extremes can cite biblical justification for the stand they take.

So as future chapters move into social issues without much, if any, Scripture to cite, maybe you can see why some churches think one way while others take almost the opposite view. But before we get into some of the more controversial topics, let's start with a look at basic morality and values. On these matters, the Bible is quite clear and we can find more to agree on.

Give Us Your Tired, Your Killers, Your Pagans . . .

First, let's affirm that Christianity is definitely a "come as you are" religion. The first verse most of us memorize (after "Jesus wept") is John 3:16, where Jesus promises that "everyone who believes in [Me] will not perish but have eternal life." The "everyone" in the verse includes, well, *everyone*. Jesus isn't speaking of just the good and pure among us.

In fact, Paul goes to the other extreme when describing the people who were flocking into the church. It isn't a pretty picture, but it shows the amazing contrast between the behavior of such people before and after their conversion to Christ. He writes: "Don't you know that those who do wrong will have no share in the kingdom of God? Don't fool yourselves. Those who indulge in sexual sin, who are idol worshipers, adulterers, male prostitutes, homosexuals, thieves, greedy people, drunkards, abusers, and swindlers—none of these will have a share in the kingdom of God. There was a time when some of you were just like that, but now your sins have been washed away, and you have been set apart for God" (1 Corinthians 6:9-11).

Doesn't this sound like a group more likely to be found in a prison holding cell rather than in the church? So how did these people go from being among Corinth's Most Wanted to become growing Christians and responsible church members? The same way any of us do—they allowed God to change them, and they began to adjust their way of thinking to conform to His.

They responded to the offer of "come as you are." They discovered that nobody is bad enough to be rejected by God. *All* are invited to receive His love, mercy, and forgiveness. At the same time, they didn't dare *stay* as they were. They realized that none of

SEE FOR YOURSELF

"Don't copy the behavior and customs of the world, but let God transform you into a new person by changing the way you think. Then you will know what God wants you to do, and you will know how good and pleasing and perfect his will really is" (Romans 12:2).

SEE FOR YOURSELF

Even the strict and legal tone of the Old Testament contains passages revealing that God is not merely a stern taskmaster with a "because I said so" answer to every question. One of the classic passages is Isaiah 55:1-7, which includes:

"Is anyone thirsty? Come and drink— even if you have no money! Come, take your choice of wine or milk—it's all free! Why spend your money on food that does not give you strength? Why pay for food that does you no good? Listen, and I will tell you where to get food that is good for the soul! . . .

"Seek the Lord while you can find him. Call on him now while he is near."

SEE FOR YOURSELF

"Unless the Lord builds a house, the work of the builders is useless" (Psalm 127:1).

140

us are good enough to take Him up on His offer of salvation without having to make some significant changes in our behavior and loyalties.

Sin is just as fatal for those of us who fudge a little on tax payments as it is for convicted rapists and murderers. Scripture is clear that *all* have sinned (Romans 3:23). None of us get a free pass to heaven based on our own merits. And since only God provides a way out of the miry gunk of sin, we need to respond by conforming to what He wants for us.

The Code of the Blessed

The Bible also provides a number of goals for us as we begin to transform ourselves to do what God desires of us. Just as the rowdy cowboys of the frontier days had a "Code of the West" to live by that tended to civilize their society to some degree, Christians have a code of behavior they should attempt to live by that tends to make them a bit less rowdy than they once were. The following qualities are to be included in any believer's moral code.

Genuine Worship (Matthew 6)

Before we even think about looking inward to fix the things that need adjusting, we need to look upward and focus on God. The biblical challenge is not to "transform yourself," but rather to "let God transform you." Certainly, there are things we can do to promote change, but the process begins and ends with God. People have tried for centuries to work hard enough to feel good about themselves, but without God's involvement in the process, all that work is for nothing.

Sadly, it's quite easy to be active in church in today's culture without being genuine in worship. We can sing at the top of our lungs, nod at all the preacher's well-prepared points, and give till it hurts. But genuine worship takes place in prayer closets and private places. It is comprised of heartfelt acts of kindness toward others and uncounted, unwitnessed good deeds. Real worship of God includes fear and trembling as well as joy and laughter. Until we approach such a level of true worship, it is doubtful that any other "transformation" in our lives will be significant.

Sexual Integrity (1 Corinthians 6:18-20)

As we tune our spiritual lives to God in love and obedience, we will almost immediately become aware of things in our lives that need attention. For many people, sexual issues will be among the first to stand out.

Perhaps now more than ever before, others will take notice of a person whose moral code includes sexual purity. You may remember that when the first church council was spelling out guidelines for the new Gentile believers, they didn't require circumcision, but they did include abstaining from sexual immorality (Acts 15:28-29). This particular New Testament guideline is broad and nonspecific. But lest we start looking for loopholes, we can turn to the Old Testament where just about every possibility is spelled out . . . and prohibited. For example, Leviticus 18 forbids sex with one's mother, his father's other wives, any sisters or half-sisters, granddaughters, aunts, daughters-in-law, both a woman and her daughter or granddaughter or sister, a neighbor's wife, and so forth. Bestiality and homosexuality are also specifically prohibited. And numerous other passages forbid fornication and/or adultery in general.

Even during the age of polygamy and concubines, the rules about sex were quite specific. And with the teaching of the New Testament came further restrictions. Anyone involved with church leadership was required to be faithful to a single wife (1 Timothy 3:2, 12). Guidelines were provided for married couples as well (1 Corinthians 7). And throughout the New Testament, proper sexual behavior is demanded.

It is hard to overemphasize the need for sexual integrity among Christians. It may seem that such behavior would come naturally, but many people have faced great temptations in this area. And when you think about it, you may see the potential problems.

Christians are sent out into the world with a message of love. Their mission is to comfort and help people who are lost and hurt-

QUESTIONS?

With all the emphasis on sexual purity, why did the Old Testament allow for multiple wives?

God's original model for marriage was one man with one woman, and the New Testament reinforces the two-becoming-one concept that becomes impossible when greater numbers get involved. Indeed, much of Old Testament chaos was a result of polygamy. Yet during Old Testament times remarriage of widows was essentially the only way for them to survive in such a male-dominated society. If two brothers were both married, and one brother died, the other brother had the responsibility to care for the widow. And perhaps caring for her would include marriage and providing her with children of her own who would be sure she was supported during her later years.

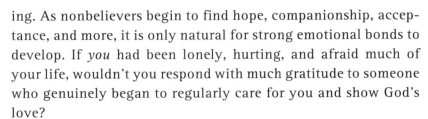

SAYS WHO?

"We may argue eloquently that 'Honesty is the best Policy'—unfortunately, the moment honesty is adopted for the sake of policy it mysteriously ceases to be honesty."—*Dorothy L. Sayers*

TRIVIA TIDBIT

Once upon a time, it wasn't a bad thing to be called a gossip. The word derives from the Old English *sibb*, meaning "relationship." So a *God-sibb* was a "kinsman in the Lord." Other older definitions of the word have included "a close and familiar friend," and "a godparent." But apparently, many of those good and Christian friendships must not have worked out, because today the word rarely has any positive connotations.

ing. As nonbelievers begin to find hope, companionship, acceptance, and more, it is only natural for strong emotional bonds to develop. If *you* had been lonely, hurting, and afraid much of your life, wouldn't you respond with much gratitude to someone who genuinely began to regularly care for you and show God's love?

Yet in the case of opposite genders, it is all too common for that loving emotional bond to short-circuit into romantic and/or sexual feelings. It takes a strong and well-balanced Christian to continue to let God's love flow to the other person without corrupting the growing relationship with something inappropriate.

In the same way that it has become something of a stereotype to hear of a psychiatrist and patient getting involved with one another, the same strong bonds create temptations in Christian relationships. And as we have seen far too often in recent years, at both national and local levels, sexual impropriety in the Christian arena can be devastating not only for the individuals involved but for the church as a whole.

Honesty (Colossians 3:9-10)

While sexual impropriety tends to attract more public attention, far more people are likely to struggle with issues of honesty. Christians are expected to maintain unquestionable integrity both in what they say and what they do. Our word should transcend oaths: our yes should mean yes, and our no should mean no (Matthew 5:33-37). Our actions should no longer be motivated by greed or self-interests. Instead, with practice, everything we say and do should be for the greater glory of God (Colossians 3:17).

Yet complete honesty is still a rare moral commodity in our society. It's simply too easy to get by with small untruths, cheating in school, fudging time sheets at work, calling in sick when we really just need a little personal time, and so forth. If we get caught, we have to pay the consequences. But what we forget is that even if we don't get caught *now*, someday we'll have to give an account to God for our not-so-Christian actions. We will eventually face the fact that no lie is little, nor is it white.

Purity of Speech (James 3)

Of course, lying is only one problem we can create with our words. On any given day, we might also catch ourselves involved with boasting, flattery, profanity, gossip, slander, insults, empty promises, and more. Each of these things is addressed in Scripture as something to be discarded along with our old, non-Christian lifestyles.

Nobody says such a feat will be easy. Indeed, James reminds us that, "No one can tame the tongue. It is an uncontrollable evil, full of deadly poison" (3:8). On Sunday we use it to sing praises to God and pray. On Monday we use it to belittle the boss behind her back, scold our kids for accidentally spilling their juice, repeat the off-color jokes we heard on *Saturday Night Live,* and so forth. Ours is a life of inconsistency, yet our goal is to become more consistently faithful in speech and actions.

Purity of Mind (Philippians 4:8)

Then again, you can't blame your tongue for simply saying what's on your mind. So in order to get to the root of any problems with our words, we must start by addressing what we allow ourselves to think about. This is why Jesus was so strong in His admonitions in the Sermon on the Mount. Snotty put-downs directed at someone else are the spiritual equivalent of murdering that person. Lustful thoughts are little different than literal adultery (Matthew 5:21-30).

This brings us back to that key verse in Romans 12:2: "Don't copy the behavior and customs of this world, but let God transform you into a new person by changing the way you think." It is no accident that this verse appears where it does. The book of Romans is filled with complex concepts and deep theology. Most of the basic Christian doctrines are addressed in the first eleven chapters. But as soon as Paul shifts from theology to practice, beginning in chapter 12, we find this crucial challenge—not to create a checklist of adherence to dozens of doctrines, but simply to allow God to change the way we think.

Most of us know from personal experience that when we think happy thoughts we tend to be happy. Conversely, if we're seething with rage toward someone, we're likely to display rage—not neces-

SEE FOR YOURSELF

"Fix your thoughts on what is true and honorable and right. Think about things that are pure and lovely and admirable. Think about things that are excellent and worthy of praise" (Philippians 4:8).

143

sarily at our mental target, but rather at the person closest at hand. That's why Paul reminds us to watch what we think. As we learn to do this, people become thrilled to be around us.

Humility (Philippians 2:5-8)

Upon becoming a Christian, some changes ought to be immediate. Certain sinful behaviors should be eliminated at once. Prayer and Bible study should begin with a new fervency. The move toward greater purity is set into motion.

Yet other goals commanded of Christians require long-term attention. Developing humility is one of them. In fact, one common problem among growing Christians is just the opposite of humility—pride. After so much Bible study and devotion, it is a powerful temptation to begin to evaluate oneself in comparison to how much other Christians know. Just because one Christian decides to memorize the book of Habakkuk and another doesn't, that doesn't mean the first is superior in any way. Such naïve and harmful comparisons are frequently made, however.

So Paul reminds the Philippians (and us) that only one perfect person ever existed. If we're going to compare ourselves to anyone, it should be to Jesus Christ. And when we do, we are reminded that Jesus set aside perfect knowledge, perfect love, and perfect comfort to leave heaven in order to come to earth and die a painful and humiliating death. He had nothing to gain personally from His action; He did it out of love for us. If we want to compare our spiritual growth to someone to see how we're doing, that's the example that is held out for us.

Humility is a much-overlooked trait—when it *can* be found. The people who are always scooting around to help people in need, picking up trash in the church parking lot, carrying groceries to ailing seniors, writing to encourage missionaries, and untold other things, are not the people who tend to get noticed in the average church. By definition, a humble person is not one who will stand up in the middle of a church service and yell, "Hey! Look at me! I'm the most humble person here!"

And unfortunately, others aren't always good at seeing past the pastors, staff members, and other high-profile workers to identify the people who humbly serve without calling attention to themselves. That's the other half of Paul's reminder: God didn't miss out on Jesus' humility and rewarded Him in unprecedented ways. Similarly, God doesn't overlook a single sincere act of humility, and He's the one who hands out the rewards. Humility may not seem to be its own reward here and now, but someday it will be acknowledged in wonderful and surprising ways.

Perfection (Matthew 5:43-48)

If you don't think perfection is a legitimate goal for Christian living, you'll have to take it up with Jesus, because it was His command: "You are to be perfect, even as your Father in heaven is perfect" (Matthew 5:48).

We all know that in this sin-soaked world of ours, perfection is literally impossible. As theologians like to point out, if we were capable of being perfect, it would have been unnecessary for Jesus to sacrifice Himself for us.

But it's not that we start out perfect—just the opposite. We start out so unaware of God's greatness and unconcerned for our eternal souls that we stumble around in sin until we are mired down like Brer Rabbit stuck to the tar baby. But when God in His wonderful grace forgives us and sets us free, our long-term goal is to become like Him. Consequently, God's salvation of a sinful person's soul is instantaneous. Yet the commitment of the person to become more and more Christ-like, approaching perfection, is a lifetime pursuit.

This call to perfection actually puts all the other goals into perspective for us. It's not that God is someday going to look at everyone's good works—honesty, sexual integrity, purity of mind and speech, worship, humility, and all the rest—to determine a cut-off point and then grade on the curve. Yet some of us seem to live as if we believe this. As long as I'm not as bad as the people around me, I must be quite the fine spiritual warrior. Not true!

We can easily deceive ourselves if we make spiritual comparisons between ourselves and other people. "Nobody's perfect" is

SAYS WHO?

"Have patience with all things, but chiefly have patience with yourself. Do not lose courage in considering your own imperfections, but instantly set about remedying them—every day begin the task anew."—*St. Francis de Sales*

SEE FOR YOURSELF

"So when we preach that Christ was crucified, the Jews are offended, and the Gentiles say it's all nonsense. But to those called by God to salvation, both Jews and Gentiles, Christ is the mighty power of God and the wonderful wisdom of God. The 'foolish' plan of God is far wiser than the wisest of human plans, and God's weakness is far stronger than the greatest of human strength" (1 Corinthians 1:23-25).

the world's most overused excuse. We tend to let a lot of our faults slide when we assume everyone else is doing them as well. But if we compare ourselves to Jesus instead, those faults continue to stand out as imperfections we need to work on. (To emphasize this point, Jesus gave the command in conjunction with another one to love our enemies. Anyone who has learned to love and pray for his or her persecutors is certainly farther along toward perfection than most.)

Don't Pity the Fool

In the grand scope of "what Christians believe," the preceding commands are only a few of the instructions provided for us in Scripture. However, a genuine Christian lifestyle involves much more than simply believing that we should go around doing good things. The point in pausing to look at these qualities is to remind ourselves that as Christians begin to apply these things to their personal lives, they live by a moral code that many people in society do not. Sometimes it makes them stand out in unpopular ways. To people who don't have the same spiritual perspective, the self-sacrificing lifestyle of Christians is foolish, incomprehensible, and maybe even downright weird.

As we move forward from this point, we need to remember that while Christians may not agree with the rest of society—or even with each other—about many contemporary issues, their opinions are very likely based on a personal moral code. One person's sense of accountability is likely to clash with another person's understanding of the depth of God's mercy and forgiveness. And both of their opinions may clash with their secular neighbors.

It will continue to be difficult to determine black and white, right and wrong in every case. Yet these issues are too important to sidestep. So let's now turn our attention to twenty-first century issues as we continue to examine what Christians believe.

Questions to Ponder and/or Discuss

1. What connections do you see between a Christian's doctrine and his or her behavior? What connections do you think the world at large expects?

2. Think about your own behavior during the past week and rate yourself in each of the following areas (1 = worst; 10 = best):

Genuine worship	1	2	3	4	5	6	7	8	9	10
Sexual integrity	1	2	3	4	5	6	7	8	9	10
Honesty	1	2	3	4	5	6	7	8	9	10
Purity of speech	1	2	3	4	5	6	7	8	9	10
Purity of mind	1	2	3	4	5	6	7	8	9	10
Humility	1	2	3	4	5	6	7	8	9	10
Perfection	1	2	3	4	5	6	7	8	9	10

3. What other qualities you would add to this list to be included in a personal moral code?

4. What example(s) have you seen lately where Christians were caught acting inappropriately? What were the consequences, if any, of the person's not adhering to the behavior expected from Christians? What lesson(s) can the church as a whole learn from this example?

"LOOK! YOU'RE JUST GOING TO HAVE TO TAKE RESPONSIBILITY FOR YOUR ACTIONS. BESIDES, YOU'RE A CLONE—YOU CAN'T BLAME YOUR PARENTS."

CHAPTER THIRTEEN

Science Friction

CREATION, CLONING, AND OTHER CASES OF SCIENCE VS. RELIGION

SOME THINGS YOU'LL DISCOVER IN THIS CHAPTER

1. General concerns in various areas where science and faith overlap

2. Some specifics about evolution theory, cloning, and cryonics

3. A few questions Christians need to consider in determining what they believe in these areas

In high school, some teenagers take quite naturally to science. For many others, science holds no allure other than being a series of classes to be endured in order to graduate. Little did most of us expect in high school, however, that as adults we would need a good working knowledge of science in order to better comprehend and/or defend our religious faith.

Historically, the church has had a love/hate relationship with science. At one point, most of the great scientific minds of the world had religious connections. The church supported their findings. And people like Copernicus faced a lot of opposition when they made bizarre claims such as saying the earth revolved around the sun rather than vice versa.

Then the pendulum swung the other direction, with many scientific seekers rejecting religious preconceptions. Science and religion parted company for a while. But recently, the two polarized camps

149

SAYS WHO?

"This fool [Copernicus] wishes to reverse the entire scheme of astronomy; but sacred Scripture tells us that Joshua commanded the sun to stand still, and not the earth."—*Martin Luther*

TRIVIA TIDBIT

A survey first conducted in 1916 was recently repeated and reported on in 1997. The study revealed that now, as then, 40 percent of scientists (biologists, physicists, and mathematicians) profess a belief in God, defined as a being who actively communicates with humankind and to whom a person can pray and expect to receive an answer. The results suggest that while the majority of scientists might not be gung-ho Christians, neither is it impossible for Christianity and science to come together in a united pursuit of truth.

have been making tentative overtures to acknowledge and respect each other's way of thinking.

The perception some people have is that essentially all true scientists have something of an anti-religion bias, but the statistics don't back up that assumption. In fact, certain scholars—both secular and Christian—have begun to complain that science is beginning to be perceived as almost a religion in itself. Like many religious concepts, much of science requires faith because it is speculative. Even while some scientists scoff at religious teachings that can't be proven, they endorse scientific theories that Christians find equally spurious. And representatives from both theology and science are calling for more mutual respect. Let science be science, and let religion be religion.

Both science and theology will always deal with mystery. Science has no answers to explain things such as values, beauty, the supernatural, and so forth. Christians feel they have found certain truth in regard to such things. And a tolerance is developing to allow room for both, though still there is much tension when certain topics are raised.

We want to look at just a few issues that fall in the shadowy area between science and religion. We aren't likely to patch up any old grievances between the two, but we at least need to be aware what we're arguing about.

You Say You Want an Evolution?

For decades now the hands-down biggest conflict between science and religion has been the evolution-vs.-creation debate. The Scopes trial took place in 1926, resulting in a slap-on-the-wrist fine of $100 for John Scopes' effrontery in teaching evolution in public schools. But the trial didn't exactly settle the matter. Since then, problems almost always arise wherever evolution and education cross paths.

Perhaps you've taken a stand on this issue without ever giving the matter much thought. So let's take a look at some of the basic beliefs on both sides of the issue.

The creationist position is based on a literal interpretation of Scripture. The creation of both the earth and of human beings was the intentional work of God, created from nothing, and on His timetable. God was involved personally and lovingly in forming both a habitat and a humanity. Humans were created in the image of God, and God Himself breathed life into them. The first people, along with the plants and animals created before them, were provided with the ability to reproduce.

The theory of evolution suggests that life was perhaps equally miraculous, but not so intentional. Billions of years ago, somewhere, somehow, the right conditions formed to generate a life force from inanimate matter. First a cell, then two, then four, and given enough time, the complexities increased until we now have a massive variety of animal species, including six billion humans.

The basic differences in creationism and evolution are too great to be resolved to any degree of satisfaction. Yet some people suggest the truth is perhaps somewhere in between the two extremes. Maybe, for example, life did indeed evolve as theorized, but at some point God stepped in and created something better than had been developed by that time. Maybe evolution was even a tool God used to create life. So we can find proponents of "scientific creationism" as well as "theistic evolution."

Evolutionists have traditionally rejected the creationist stance because they prefer answers based on science rather than faith. Yet recently the original theory of evolution has been questioned by certain scientists and deep thinkers. One problem is that no matter how dearly one wants to believe that life evolved, the theory never satisfactorily explains how it *began.*

And even if you want to concede that a one-celled form of life *somehow* came to exist at a point in prehistory, it's simply too much a stretch of science (not to mention the imagination) to think that a life form as complex as humans has evolved so quickly. Even going with the oldest estimates of the age of the earth, the math simply doesn't work when you study how long is required for a series of genetic mutations that would change a paramecium into Arnold Schwarzenegger. Many authorities suggest the earth is billions of

SEE FOR YOURSELF

"And the Lord God formed a man's body from the dust of the ground and breathed into it the breath of life. And the man became a living person. . . . And the Lord God said, 'It is not good for the man to be alone. I will make a companion who will help him.' . . . So the Lord God caused Adam to fall into a deep sleep. He took one of Adam's ribs and closed up the place from which he had taken it. Then the Lord God made a woman from the rib and brought her to Adam" (Genesis 2:7, 18, 21-22).

SAYS WHO?

"You can only find truth with logic if you have already found truth without it."
—G. K. Chesterton

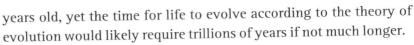

TRIVIA TIDBIT

An Irish churchman named James Ussher (1581–1656) traced the genealogies and events of the Bible and arrived at the "fact" that Creation took place on October 22, 4004 B.C. Some people still support his findings.

years old, yet the time for life to evolve according to the theory of evolution would likely require trillions of years if not much longer.

So lately, many in the scientific community have come to accept an "intelligent designer" theory of creation. They don't necessarily concede that God gets the credit (though some do). But they allow for the possibility that not everything happened by chance. Maybe a meteorite hit the earth that contained some kind of life from another planet. Maybe the residents of the as-yet-undiscovered Formeyanmy Galaxy were vacationing here and left behind some alien DNA that got things started. Maybe the universe itself is infused with a life force. When you're speculating on such a grand scale, anything could have happened. Yet while the "intelligence" that got things started remains undefined, more and more people are seemingly willing to acknowledge that something or someone certainly must have acted in earth's past.

And while scientists debate their various theories, so do Christians. The ones who want to allow for some kind of evolution have a hard time answering others who say, "Even if that explains Adam, how about *Eve*?" Even if God chose to use evolution to create His first human, that's not how the second one came into existence (if Scripture is to be believed).

Then there's the perpetual discussion about whether the "days" of creation were literal 24-hour periods or longer periods of time. Arguments for both can be made. But the proponents of the literal 24-hour days are left with a "young earth" that is thousands, rather than billions, of years old. The fossil deposits and carbon-dated antiquities have to be explained as a miraculous invention of God much like the wine Jesus created from water. Just as Jesus skipped the process of fermentation and went straight to the finished product, perhaps God did something similar in the creation of the earth. Others feel that God would not promote such a deceptive illusion.

No one, neither creationists nor evolutionists nor "intelligent designer" proponents, can provide irrefutable answers for how life began. Creationists don't need provable answers because they have faith in the integrity of the Scriptures. Evolution scientists don't require absolute proof because they are accustomed to working

with theories that make lots of sense to them yet lack enough evidence to become scientific laws. And with both groups satisfied with their beliefs, neither side is likely to enlist a lot of converts from the other. It's those of us who may not have given the matter a lot of thought who need to be careful to weigh all the evidence before making a hasty decision based on a catchy slogan or brief statement from one group or the other.

Evolutionists scoff at Christian "myths" of creation. And Christians strongly oppose evolution because if they can't trust the very first story of the Bible, what does that suggest about the *rest* of the Good book? Scientists who also have chosen to be Christians are left to search for truth in both areas as they attempt to fill the holes in both their knowledge and their faith.

A Clone Again (Unnaturally)

Now let's move from the concept of being created in the image of God to being created in the image of oneself. One of the most rapid and startling trends of the recent past is the advancement of cloning experimentation. Long a favorite plot of science fiction stories, the concept has suddenly become alarmingly real.

The proponents of cloning give good reasons for pursuing it. They suggest that couples at risk of producing children with hereditary problems can greatly reduce potential problems, and infertile couples can have children of their own. Just as we're learning to breed healthier livestock through cloning, perhaps the same progress could be applied to human beings.

In addition, we can restore the depleted ranks of endangered species. Cloning, though not without certain risks, is not as dangerous as other accepted medical procedures and might provide many more organs that could be used for transplants. So in light of these worthwhile causes, why not pursue all the possibilities full steam ahead?

The success of this process made big news when it worked with Dolly the sheep in 1997. It has also worked with other animals, including pigs, and current tests are being conducted with monkeys. Yet the successes we hear about have occurred only after the

QUESTIONS?

With all the evolution vs. creation debate, is there an official stance for "what Christians believe"?

Not officially, but most Christians probably include Creation among their basic beliefs. If we forego the biblical creation account, we also lose the story of a personal and knowable God whose image we bear. That's not something many Christians are willing to give up. And in regard to the enigmas of science that remain unanswered, Christians will continue to search for additional information that builds upon the truth they already accept.

QUESTIONS?

How does cloning work?

In theory, the process is quite simple. You start with a donor embryo and separate out the cells. Perhaps you modify the cells to create just what you want under controlled conditions. Then you remove the chromosomes from an unfertilized egg and use an electrical current to bond your designated cells with the egg. You're sure to include a nucleus so the cells will form an embryo. And finally, you plant the embryo into a female of the species. When the female gives birth, the new baby is an exact genetic duplicate of the donor.

TRIVIA TIDBIT

A few years ago an unnamed couple donated $2.3 million to Texas A & M University to clone their beloved dog, Missy. The university had already done a lot of research in cloning livestock. In addition to providing a clone for Missy, the project was expected to be valuable in learning to replicate dogs that show an exceptional ability as guides or rescue animals.

deaths of many embryos and newborn "clones." And scientists have yet to see how well cloned animals will endure the stresses of the normal life cycle. All the shortcomings of cloning add to the concern whenever the topic of *human* cloning is mentioned.

Opponents suggest that cloning is at the pinnacle of recent attempts of scientists to "play God" by rerouting or short-circuiting the natural design of how things were created to be. On a medical/scientific basis, they oppose cloning because it could potentially introduce new problems into the human gene pool. Extremists foresee the eventual misuse of cloning to create a subclass of people genetically engineered for slavery, warfare, or other unpopular functions. And since we know so little about the lasting effects of cloning, concern for the young cloned individuals is a major issue.

But even stronger than the medical protests are social ones. If you were a cloned member of your family amid several other biological siblings, might you be likely to feel inferior to some degree? Would parents show just as much affection for a cloned child as for a "natural" one? Again, this mentality has been prominent in science fiction looks into the future. Clones are frequently portrayed as little more than robots. And even though this would not necessarily be reality, it is a common perception to be overcome.

Scientists have recently mapped the human genome, yet they also assure us that genes are only one factor contributing to who a person is to become. For example, a gene for musical ability is never likely to flourish if the child is denied access to an instrument and/or adequate instruction. Studies with "identical" twins show that at times they can demonstrate tremendous differences in personality, talent, and other factors. The same should be true of genetically identical clones as well.

Lots of people, including scientists, are opposed to human cloning. The politicians are trying to do their part by banning any kind of cloning where humans are involved. But to add to the debate is a new area of study called "therapeutic cloning." The purpose is to generate a cloned embryo of someone—not to create another person, but to provide exact-match stem cells that could be used to cure Parkinson's disease, diabetes, and numerous other maladies.

Some people are aghast to consider creating embryos only to destroy them. Others, however, hold out hope for this method of helping people who are seriously ill and see no other options for a cure. A significant number of scientists who oppose reproductive cloning of humans are in favor of continued research in the area of therapeutic cloning. The debates are certain to continue as representatives of science, law, and theology remain involved.

Cloning advocates like to remind us that as a society, we have resisted many of the previous great scientific advances. Organ transplants were at first perceived to be morbid and gruesome. In-vitro fertilization was (and perhaps still is) condemned by some, though it has provided much joy for other women who had lost hope of conceiving a child of their own. So just because someone else takes a slightly different path than we did to get here, they say, once we're together we should make the best of it.

SEE FOR YOURSELF

"Our earthly bodies, which die and decay, will be different when they are resurrected, for they will never die. Our bodies now disappoint us, but when they are raised, they will be full of glory. They are weak now, but when they are raised, they will be full of power. They are natural human bodies now, but when they are raised, they will be spiritual bodies. For just as there are natural bodies, so also there are spiritual bodies" (1 Corinthians 15:42-44).

Is It Getting Cold in Here?

Cryogenics (or cryogeny) is a branch of physics dealing with very cold temperatures. Perhaps you've seen a television science wizard dip a fresh and fragrant rose into a container of liquid nitrogen, and then smash it into tiny bits like fragile porcelain.

Extreme cold can do amazing things. One of the things it does is postpone tissue decomposition. That's why if it's going to be a few weeks before you cook that raw hamburger you bought today, you might want to stick it in the freezer for a while. And going a few additional steps further with this phenomenon of extreme cold has come the field of cryonics.

Cryonics is the storage of dead, diseased bodies in very cold temperatures with the anticipation of bringing them back to life after a cure has been found for whatever it was that ailed them. Sometimes only the head is put "on ice" with the expectation of hooking up with a better body somewhere down the line. Your loved ones can pay rent on your cryonic chamber just as they would any other storage facility, or you can make other financial arrangements prior to your demise.

SAYS WHO?

"Science without religion is lame, religion without science is blind."
—*Albert Einstein*

So far, cryonics is primarily a theoretical science. We hear a lot of hopes and speculations for what may be possible some day, but so far we haven't heard a lot of testimonials from people who have come back to life thanks to a lengthy ice nap in the deep freeze.

For Christians, the questions raised by cryonics should be obvious: What are we hoping to achieve? Or even more relevant, what are we trying to *avoid*?

Web sites for cryonics companies dangle tantalizing words like *immortality* to lure potential customers. But an extreme fear of or resistance to death is counter to Christian faith. From a biblical perspective, it is *this* life that is sick, diseased, and imperfect. Yes, Jesus promises us "life in all its fullness" (John 10:10), but if we're geared up for this life only, we are pitiable, if not pitiful (1 Corinthians 15:19).

The life Jesus holds out for believers is *eternal* life. It doesn't seem logical to go to great extremes to avoid the transition from here-and-now to forever-and-ever. Jesus awaits us in a place of perfect love, but death is the doorway from here to there. Why try so hard to postpone the trip in a cryonic chamber? Given the choice between sub-zero temperatures and the warmth of the love of God, it seems odd to decide to chill out.

When the By-Products of Progress Are People

Evolution vs. Creation. Cloning. Cryonics.

These are only a few of the potential sources of controversy that arise when science and religion begin to intersect. We could explore other specifics, but our time might be better spent considering a more general question. As science continues to complicate our lives in ways both wonderful and awkward, how should we respond?

For example, suppose you've gone on record as vehemently against human cloning, yet science moves right ahead against your wishes. What if you discover one day that the new family next door are all the result of human cloning experiments? How do you respond?

Just as Christians in the past have sometimes been guilty of neglecting the spiritual needs of minorities, will the same be true in the future? For many years, African-American slaves were perceived more as property than people, and were therefore not accorded basic human rights. At times women have struggled to have any semblance of equality. Will the same be true of human clones or cryonically restored people? Will such individuals be treated with fear, suspicion, antagonism, apathy, or worse?

This seems like a silly consideration right now. Yet as science continues to advance, we might be faced with these or similar questions at some point in the future. We can bury our heads in the church and not dare to think about such things, but that won't ensure that scientific progress will grind to a halt.

Isn't it the mission and responsibility of Christians to address the spiritual needs of those around them? If and when human cloning takes place, will we be at the forefront to speak up for the rights of the individuals, or will we be so repelled by the concept that we repel the *people* involved? Regardless of how people come to be in our presence, and whether or not we feel it *should* have happened, Christians need to extend God's love to those people.

If you *do* discover your neighbor was cloned instead of born as you were, it might be a bit rude to scream, "You freak!" every time you see him. Like any other "minority," he needs your love and support.

Or in a more likely consideration, your neighbor is probably not a human clone, but he might well be a believer in evolution. So does *that* negate your responsibility to love him? It is fine to have our own strongly held views about faith and science. But if we allow a difference in personal philosophies and doctrines to cause us to reject other *people*, perhaps we need to review exactly what we say we believe.

What Christians believe is that the eternal souls of other people are more important than their scientific, political, or religious opinions. We may not sway anyone's thinking by extending God's love to him or her. But the sure way *not* to make a positive difference is to *withhold* love.

SAYS WHO?

"Science is a first-rate piece of furniture for a man's upper chamber if he has common sense on the ground floor."
—*Oliver Wendell Holmes, Sr.*

Showing love to an evolutionist, an atheist, or a human clone does not diminish in the least our own devotion to God. Indeed, we are likely to need a special portion of God's strength and courage to do so. As science continues to create strange new opportunities, the church should be there to make the most of them.

Questions to Ponder and/or Discuss

1. When it comes to your interest in (and comprehension of) science, who are you more like?

   Archimedes (I do my best thinking in the bathtub.)

   Copernicus (I believe what I believe, and I don't care what anyone else thinks.)

   Galileo (My idea of scientific experimentation is dropping heavy things off of tall buildings.)

   Marie Curie (Vive la women!)

   Albert Einstein (I love to ponder things such as "the speed of light squared.")

   Other:

2. Have you had any conversations about evolution with someone who disagreed with you? Would you classify them as dialogs, debates, or arguments? How did they turn out? What would you do differently next time?

3. What are your personal feelings toward subjects such as cloning and cryonics? Do you think limits should be set for what scientists are allowed to experiment with? Who do you think should determine those limits?

CHAPTER FOURTEEN

Wanted Dead? Or Alive?

ABORTION, SUICIDE, CAPITAL PUNISHMENT

To be or not to be?

Shakespeare may have summarized the problem succinctly through the lips of Hamlet, but we know the dilemma of being caught between life and death had been around long before that. The Bible makes us aware of a number of suicides. Socrates had been given hemlock to drink as a form of capital punishment. And already centuries of wars, executions, Crusades, plagues, and other events had repeatedly raised questions about death and how it might relate to morality, religion, and eternity. Hamlet didn't mind what he perceived to be the long, comforting sleep of death. But he wasn't too keen about what he might dream during that lengthy sleep. In his words, "Ay, there's the rub; for in that sleep of death what dreams may come, when we have shuffled off this mortal coil, must give us pause." Then he drifts off into a soliloquy about fardels, bare bodkins, and making quietus. (Sounds as if he *was* quite the confused young Dane.)

No doubt about it, when death enters the discussion, the dialog

SAYS WHO

"Any man's death diminishes me, because I am involved in mankind; and therefore never send to know for whom the bell tolls; it tolls for thee."
—John Donne

usually takes on a more serious and perhaps confusing tone. We all have opinions, religious beliefs, and other priorities that we feel strongly about. But when personally confronted with some of the harsher issues of life, we see exactly how committed we are to what we *say* we believe. Fortunately, we aren't faced with this choice very often. But as we now approach contemporary topics that involve dying, we need to be sensitive about the finality of death. While *we* or those we love may never face such conditions, we must try to empathize with those who do.

Suicide: Whose Life Is It Anyway?

In many of these issues, opinions will be strongly divided. But in the official record of "what Christians believe" about suicide, most oppose it. However, the Bible never actually comes out and says, "Thou shalt not kill thyself." In taking a stand against suicide, the church usually cites the prohibition against murder, and then applies it to murdering oneself.

This view is given credence if we take a closer look at the biblical accounts of suicides. We discover a number of people who anticipated receiving justice for sins they had committed, and they pre-empted such unpleasant thoughts by taking their own lives. Theirs were acts of desperation rather than noble sacrifices.

Suicides in the Bible

- King Saul drifted away from God, lost a key battle, and killed himself rather than let the Philistines take him (1 Samuel 31:4).
- Saul's armor bearer wasn't willing to live if Saul didn't (1 Samuel 31:5).
- A royal advisor named Ahithophel regretted that his defection from David's side to Absalom's side didn't turn out so well (2 Samuel 17:23).
- Wicked King Zimri saw that his throne was about to taken from him by force, so he burned down the royal palace around him (1 Kings 16:18).

- And in the best known suicide of all, Judas Iscariot killed himself when reality set in about what he had done to Jesus (Matthew 27:1-5; Acts 1:18-19).

These were by no means glorious, romanticized deaths. They were impulsive, final acts of desperate men. Some people include Samson as a casualty of suicide, but others consider his final act more as a heroic self-sacrifice against Israel's enemies (Judges 16:23-31).

Scripture also provides a few examples of assisted suicide, as is the case of another judge—something of a wild and crazy leader—named Abimelech. While he was attempting to burn down a tower holding a number of people, a woman dropped a millstone from the top and cracked his thick skull. Realizing he was about to die and not wanting to be remembered for such an inglorious death, he had his armor-bearer spear him to death with a sword. (Yet Scripture ironically records the behind-the-scenes story of the lady who conked him on the head. See Judges 9:46-55.)

In addition to biblical accounts of suicides are historical ones. Perhaps the most dramatic is the story of Masada, an outpost in the Judean desert where the Jewish Zealots made a final stand against the Romans in A.D. 73. When their defeat was imminent, they opted for mass suicide rather than surrender. According to the historian, Josephus, they drew lots to select ten men who would kill their group of 960. When that gruesome job was done, one of the ten killed the other nine, and then himself.

Yet while the issue of suicide has been evident throughout history and perhaps even glorified at times, it has rarely been a culturally accepted practice. It is almost always a sign of hopelessness, which from a Christian perspective leaves God out of the picture. Hope should be a quality in the life of every growing Christian and should be strongest during times of suffering.

Another major concern for Christians is the belief that God is the source of life to begin with. If we believe that, then who are *we* to end prematurely what God has given us? We usually think of marriage when we read, "What God has joined together, let man not separate" (Matthew 19:6, NIV). But if we believe that God gives *us*

SEE FOR YOURSELF

"We work hard and suffer much in order that people will believe the truth, for our hope is in the living God, who is the Savior of all people, and particularly of those who believe" (1 Timothy 4:10).

TRIVIA TIDBIT

At this writing, Surgeon General David Satcher has just released a plan to address the problem of suicide in the United States. He is being credited as the first person in his position to focus so intensely on the subjects of suicide and mental health in general.

SAYS WHO?

"The man who, in a fit of melancholy, kills himself today, would have wished to live if he'd waited a week." —*Voltaire*

life just as He breathed the breath of life into Adam, then we dare not take the initiative to separate ourselves from that life flow.

Suicide has become the third leading cause of death in the 15-24 age group, sixth among children ages 5-14, and eighth overall. Out of half a million suicide attempts each year, five thousand or more teenagers succeed in killing themselves. As adults we see the irreparable tragedy of losing youngsters to a period of depression and a single moment of too-great despair. We come to see that essentially any problem, given a month or a year or *some* amount of time, is capable of being solved. And we mourn the forceful and final act of another's suicide.

Yet we may then come full circle and begin to defend suicide for the elderly or terminally ill. We begin to use terms such as "quality of life" to set standards beyond which we justify an early death. Some defend this dichotomy; others consider it hypocritical. How can we tell a depressed teenager to hang in there because things are going to get better and then reach to pull the plug on a suffering, aged parent?

Of course, when examined on a case-by-case basis, the matter of suicide rarely is simple. Who can blame someone in constant physical agony for wanting to hasten death? After all, death is going to come sometime, sooner or later. Why not sooner? From a purely spiritual perspective, death isn't something we should fear. In a particularly honest moment, the Apostle Paul even confessed that he had given the matter some thought: "I'm torn between two desires: Sometimes I want to live, and sometimes I long to go and be with Christ. That would be far better for me, but it is better for you that I live" (Philippians 1:23-24).

Perhaps Paul's explanation provides the best possible anti-suicide logic. As human beings, and particularly as believers, we have an obligation to look beyond our own feelings and concerns. We see in the aftermath of suicide what a toll it takes on the friends and loved ones who remain. Suicide is perhaps the ultimate act of selfishness. Young people who take their own lives rob their families of potential decades of growth and affection. And older people who are quick to kick up the morphine drip beyond the point of no return deny future generations of what doctors might learn to better treat someone else.

To be sure, everyone's life contains a fair amount of suffering. In some cases, the amount of suffering is definitely *unfair*. Yet in the context of eternity, life—as well as suffering—is short.

Like Job, we cry out in confusion and disappointment. Like Job, the best human advice we receive might seem to be, "Curse God and die!" Like Job, we may be unaware that God sees our every injustice and hears our every cry as all we feel is pain and frustration. And like Job, if we can persevere through the trials, God will eventually restore a sense of stability to life and reward our faithfulness.

Some insist that to opt for suicide at any point in life is to turn one's back on God and deny that He will do as He has promised. Others say you need to be in a situation where you have to watch the awful, endless suffering of a loved one before you can make such a determination.

Opinions vary as to the eternal consequences of suicide. In the Catholic tradition, sins such as murder and blasphemy are "mortal sins," which can lead to eternal punishment if not pardoned at the time of death. And obviously, no one has the opportunity to confess the sin of suicide. Most Protestants consider suicide forgivable if committed by someone who has professed faith in Jesus. Another common opinion suggests that no one who commits suicide is sound of mind, and therefore such people should not be judged by the same standards as, say, a cold-blooded, intentional murderer.

When we are faced with the irreversible pain and tragedy of the suicide of a loved one, we can only trust that God is perfectly fair and just. He will do nothing inappropriate or undeserved, and He will see us through the emotional chaos we are certain to struggle through.

QUESTIONS?

Isn't trusting God during hard times pretty much the same as "wishful thinking"?

At perhaps the bleakest point in the Old Testament—after Israel and Judah had been taken into exile by hostile and powerful opponents—God's promises to His people were sure and certain. Here's just one example: " 'For I know the plans I have for you,' says the Lord. 'They are plans for good and not for disaster, to give you a future and a hope' " (Jeremiah 29:11).

It is when we run out of all other alternatives that God is able to prove Himself to us beyond any doubt. Faith may not be our *only* option during such times, but it is certainly the best one.

TRIVIA TIDBIT

It is frequently advised that people who lose close friends or family members to suicide should receive competent counseling for a period of time. Recent cases show that young people, especially, are sometimes prone to attempt "copycat" suicides after a friend takes his or her own life.

Abortion: A Womb with a Number of Views

Somehow most "discussions" about abortion tend to quickly degenerate into slogans and/or screaming matches between "pro-life" and "pro-choice." But the issue is not actually so easily delineated.

SAYS WHO?

"To hinder a birth is merely speedier man-killing; nor does it matter whether you take away a life that is born, or destroy one that is coming to the birth. That is a man which is going to be one; you have the fruit already in its seed."—
Tertullian (160–225)

Lots of people who personally oppose abortion might also concede that women (and men) should have the right to make their own moral and physical choices. After all, this is America where we take our freedom rather seriously. And indeed, statistics reflect that a majority of people in the United States have "serious reservations" about abortion, yet a majority are also in favor of ensuring it remains a legal right for women.

It would also be a gross overstatement to claim that everyone who favors abortion under certain circumstances should carry the implicated label of "anti-life." It is not unheard of for those who work with very young girls who are scared and pregnant—perhaps bearing the child of a rapist or family member—to soften a prior intense opposition to abortion. After looking into thousands of these young girls' faces, it can be difficult to take an absolute stand against abortion, even while clinging to a personal commitment to the sanctity of life. In contrast, it's rather easy to maintain a hard-line stand if we never take a close look at the harsh realities of the problem.

Several crucial factors come into play whenever the topic of abortion is raised. One is the often-debated issue of exactly when life begins. Many Christians have a firm conviction that life begins at conception. They are fond of quoting biblical passages that reflect God's future plans for as-yet-unborn people. Here are a few of the passages frequently used:

- "You made all the delicate, inner parts of my body and knit me together in my mother's womb. . . . You watched me as I was being formed in utter seclusion, as I was woven together in the dark of the womb" (Psalm 139:13, 15).
- "The Lord gave me a message. He said, 'I knew you before I formed you in your mother's womb. Before you were born I set you apart and appointed you as my spokesman to the world' " (Jeremiah 1:4-5).
- "In a loud voice [Elizabeth] exclaimed [to Mary]: 'Blessed are you among women, and blessed is the child you will bear! . . .

As soon as the sound of your greeting reached my ears, the baby in my womb leaped for joy' " (Luke 1:42, 44, NIV).

In addition to these passages are a number of prophecies that a woman would conceive a child who would be special. Such assurances were made to Sarah (Genesis 18:9-14), Samson's mother (Judges 13:3-5), Mary the mother of Jesus (Luke 1:26-38), and others. Those who believe Scripture often come to the conclusion that each and every child to be born has a God-foreseen future and fits snugly into God's overall plan for humanity. Abortion, therefore, is not merely the removal of a not-yet-viable embryo, but rather the loss of a very real person as well as all that that unique child of God might have done in his or her lifetime.

Advocates for abortion don't agree that life begins at conception. It then becomes a matter of determining exactly *when* the fetus transforms from a growing cluster of cells into a state advanced enough to be considered a person.

The abortion issue was taken to the Supreme Court in the Roe vs. Wade case of 1973. The court ruled that during the first trimester of pregnancy, a state cannot regulate abortions at all as long as a licensed doctor oversees the procedure. During the second trimester, the state was allowed to refuse an abortion if the woman's health was at risk. And during the third trimester, the state could refuse all abortions except for those needed in order to save the life of the mother. These determinations were made on the basis that the fetus usually becomes "viable" (capable of living outside the uterus) at about 28 weeks, but sometimes as early as 24 weeks.

The Roe vs. Wade decision initiated an increase in abortions, as well as in numerous state attempts to restrict abortions and subsequent hearings in the Supreme Court. Now 30 years later, anti-abortion advocates are still attempting to have the Roe vs. Wade decision overturned. Abortion is widespread, yet only about a third of the population desires stricter abortion laws, with 64 percent satisfied with current laws or willing to have less strict regulations.

QUESTIONS?

The Roe vs. Wade case is cited a lot, but what were the specifics?

"Jane Roe" was a pseudonym to ensure the privacy of a Texas woman named Norma McCorvey. When denied an abortion in 1969, she sued the Dallas County district attorney, Henry Wade, hoping to challenge the law. The case went all the way to the Supreme Court, who ruled that states must allow women to have abortions during the first three months of pregnancy. And during the second three months, the state is only allowed to ban the procedure if it might endanger the mother's health. Two of the nine justices dissented.

TRIVIA TIDBIT

Norma McCorvey ("Jane Roe" of Roe vs. Wade) made the news in 1995 when she was baptized by the fundamentalist leader of a prominent anti-abortion group. At the time she had softened her stance on abortion. She still believed a woman should be able to have an abortion during her first trimester, but no longer supported abortion during the second trimester. She also quit her job as marketing director for a pro-choice women's clinic in Dallas.

TRIVIA TIDBIT

Recent research revealed that one in six Americans report being responsible for a pregnancy that ended in abortion. Up to 25 percent of all pregnancies in the United States are aborted, and as many as 43 percent of all women will have an abortion during their lifetimes. Another study found that 78 percent of respondents believed people can be both religious and in favor of abortion rights. As of 1999, an estimated 38 million to 40 million legal abortions had been conducted—an average of almost 1.5 million each year since 1973.

And as should be expected, each side challenges the other in regard to its stand on the topic. Some of those who say life begins at conception and are strongly pro-life are willing to undergo in vitro fertilization in order to have children of their own. The process, however, involves fertilizing a number of eggs, some of which are eventually destroyed or used for experimentation. If life indeed begins at the initial fertilization, the disposal of single-celled eggs can be equated (by opponents) with abortion at other early stages before the fetus is fully developed.

Abortion advocates are coming under fire for callous disregard for human life when an abortion attempt results in a live birth. A nurse at a Chicago hospital recently reported how babies who were supposed to be aborted but lived were simply wrapped in a blanket and left to die. Sometimes they live for hours before dying from lack of attention. This accepted method of "treatment" seems barbaric to many who oppose abortion. Even if life doesn't begin at conception, it certainly should begin when a baby comes out of the womb and starts breathing on its own.

The still-being-debated issue is how to determine the rights of everyone involved. No one wants to deny the rights of a pregnant woman. But abortion opponents want to consider the rights of the unborn as well. Pregnant women can speak for themselves. In addition, they frequently have powerful political lobbies behind them. Pro-life activists want to provide corresponding rights for the unborn.

And to add to the controversy is the recent approval of the "abortion pill," also known as RU-486 or mifepristone. This pill can be prescribed to terminate "early pregnancy" (up to 49 days after the beginning of the woman's last menstrual period). It's too soon to determine what effect this will have on abortion numbers in the United States. Some people expect a massive increase. However, the numbers following European release of the drug, while reflecting a bit of a rise, did not skyrocket as feared.

The emotions involved in both the pro-choice and pro-life camps are so strong that the issue is never likely to be resolved to everyone's mutual satisfaction. In most cases, Christians will oppose abortion. Yet in the zeal to promote what Christians believe, we need to be aware that the problem of abortion may have hit close to home for many people within earshot. And perhaps we should remind ourselves that we also believe in love, forgiveness, and compassion.

Capital Punishment: Life Sentence vs. Death Sentence

Compassion also comes into play as we begin to examine various opinions concerning capital punishment. Critics of conservative Christians tend to berate them because so many are strongly against abortion yet just as strongly *for* capital punishment. They want to know how the same person can be so pro-life in one case and pro-death in the next.

Christians are much more widely divided on this issue than on others we've been discussing. Although we begin with essentially the same deep respect for the sanctity of life, disagreements arise over how to apply and maintain those convictions in a legal sense.

For those in favor of capital punishment, the same passion that fuels strong anti-abortion feelings also motivates a powerful desire for justice when someone displays callous disregard for another's life. Because of the irreplaceable value of human life, many Christians are happy to follow the Old Testament policy: The *intentional* taking of another's life would result in the death of the murderer. Other punishments were established for accidental killings. But because life is so precious, the deliberate taking of a life would (and should) result in the death of the killer.

Other Christians, however, feel that we need not act so harshly in response to capital crimes. They point to people on Death Row who have religious conversions and a change of attitude that is clearly evident. Why go through with the execution of someone who is repentant beyond a shadow of a doubt?

Such opponents of the death penalty also use Scripture to support their beliefs. The same law that required "life for life" also demanded

SAYS WHO?

"The greatest destroyer of peace is abortion because if a mother can kill her own child what is left for me to kill you and you to kill me? There is nothing between." —*Mother Teresa*

TRIVIA TIDBIT

Abortion is by no means a new problem for the church. Ancient Jewish law forbade abortion, allowing it only when a woman's life was at stake. For several centuries, abortion was acceptable in Europe as long as it occurred prior to "animation," the point at which the church determined the fetus received a soul (between 40 and 80 days after conception). In 1869, Pope Pius IX ruled against any abortion after conception, and in 1895 the Catholic Church took a stand against any form of abortion. The Catholic position still rejects all abortion, allowing only for cases of indirect abortion where the fetus dies as a result of medical efforts to save the mother's life.

SEE FOR YOURSELF

"But if any harm results, then the offender must be punished according to the injury. If the result is death, the offender must be executed. If an eye is injured, injure the eye of the person who did it. If a tooth gets knocked out, knock out the tooth of the person who did it. Similarly, the payment must be hand for hand, foot for foot, burn for burn, wound for wound, bruise for bruise" (Exodus 21:23-25).

SAYS WHO?

"Executions, far from being useful examples to the survivors, have, I am persuaded, a quite contrary effect, by hardening the heart they ought to terrify. Besides the fear of an ignominious death, I believe, never deterred anyone from the commission of a crime, because, in committing it, the mind is roused to activity about present circumstances." —Mary Wollstonecraft

168

eye for eye, tooth for tooth, and so forth. Yet this was the very passage quoted by Jesus in the Sermon on the Mount as He challenged His listeners to apply a greater level of mercy and forgiveness in their relationships (Matthew 5:38-48). Yes, human life is important, but eternal life is even more so. Showing undeserved compassion is what sets Christian relationships apart from other relationships. So when Christians speak out strongly for the death penalty, some people feel that portrays them in a rather negative light.

While we're on the topic of the Sermon on the Mount, do we dare remind ourselves that Jesus also equated intense anger and name-calling with literal murder (Matthew 5:21-22)? So when someone sees a person on Death Row and mutters, "I could pull the switch on that guy myself!" to what extent does God differentiate between the person's anger and slander and the convicted criminal's act of murder? Even in such matters of justice, Christians are cautioned to be careful about their attitudes.

In addition, it might be pointed out that God didn't immediately put to death the first murderer. When Cain was concerned for his life after killing Abel, God even protected him (Genesis 4:13-15).

Of course, it is difficult to feel compassion or show mercy for people who show no remorse whatsoever. Numerous criminals have gone to their deaths defiant until the end. Yet some people feel that it's never too late for the person to change as long as he or she is living. To take the person's life might well preempt a profession of faith later on.

So if the question is, "What do Christians believe about capital punishment?" the best possible answer is, "It depends on whom you ask." Good Christian people hold strong opinions at both extremes, and many others are somewhere in between, seeing the logic of both sides and not yet reaching any personal conclusions.

For many believers, these issues are little more than philosophical mindplay. We may not know anyone on Death Row. Perhaps we've escaped knowing anyone who committed suicide. Maybe we don't even know anyone who has had an abortion (at least, not that we know of). In such cases, it's relatively easy to take a strong stand and stick to it.

However, with the sheer statistics on suicide and abortion, the majority of us are not likely to be shielded from these tragedies forever. And when forced to confront a situation that involves someone we love dearly, we may discover our beliefs challenged.

Whether or not we confront these things personally, we need to remember (as we did at the end of the previous chapter) that people are more important to God than issues. People should be more important to us, as well. The most vehement opponent of abortion, if a Christian, should be willing to embrace a hurting and remorseful *person* who has undergone the despised procedure. As we scowl at those living on Death Row, can we force ourselves to look at our children and remember that those killers were once not unlike our own kids? Can we at least relate to the grief of their parents, spouses, and others who will also be affected by the final act of justice?

To be sure, these are hard questions we're dealing with. Unless we are quite convinced that we're 100 percent right, we ought to allow a degree of tolerance for the opinions of others. And as we move on to the next chapter, the questions are only going to get harder.

SAYS WHO?

"God asks no man whether he will accept life. This is not the choice. You must take it. The only question is how."
—*Henry Ward Beecher*

Questions to Ponder and/or Discuss

1. What is the closest you have been to someone on Death Row? To someone considering an abortion? To someone who has attempted suicide or the family of someone who committed suicide?

2. What lessons did you learn in each of the situations you have been personally involved with (even to a small extent)?

3. If you were solely in control of the lawmaking process, what laws would you pass in regard to suicide, abortion, and capital punishment? (Be as specific as possible.)

4. Conduct an informal survey among other people at work or in your neighborhood to get their opinions about the topics of this chapter. In what ways do you agree with them? Do you hold a minority opinion in contrast to any of their strongly held beliefs?

CHAPTER FIFTEEN

Gender Specifics

HOMOSEXUALITY; WOMEN'S PLACE IN THE CHURCH

It has been said that there are two kinds of people: those who tend to divide people into two groups, and those who don't. The tongue-in-cheek comment is something of a put-down directed at the trend of attempting to oversimplify things. And perhaps nowhere do we find ourselves in more trouble than when we attempt to declare that men are one way, and women are another.

There are a few crucial physical distinctions, of course, for which many of us are quite happy. But beyond that, how much can we polarize the two genders? Men may be from Mars and women from Venus, as the popular pundits express it. But sometimes men and women are *many* worlds apart, and other times they seem to be so similar that any "space" between them is undetectable.

When it comes to what Christians believe, what are the appropriate roles for men and women? Again, you'll get a lot of different answers to this question. The traditional viewpoint is based on the black and white teaching of Scripture where a number of clear-cut "rules" for appropriate behavior of women are provided. Yet some

"Whatever women do, they must do twice as well as men to be thought half as good. Luckily, this is not difficult." —*Charlotte Whitton, former mayor of Ottawa*

"Whatever you say against women, they are better creatures than men, for men were made of clay, but woman was made of man."—*Jonathan Swift*

people argue that the Bible also provides rules for slaves. Just as the culture at the time tolerated slavery as well as the submission of women to men doesn't mean that either practice is ideal for modern society.

You're Sub-Missin' the Point

Let's first look at a few of the specific biblical passages before we get into the rebuttal arguments. In regard to how husband and wife should relate within marriage, a frequently quoted passage is Ephesians 5:21-28:

> And further, you will submit to one another out of reverence for Christ. You wives will submit to your husbands as you do to the Lord. For a husband is the head of his wife as Christ is the head of his body, the church; he gave his life to be her Savior. As the church submits to Christ, so you wives must submit to your husbands in everything.
>
> And you husbands must love your wives with the same love Christ showed the church. He gave up his life for her to make her holy and clean, washed by baptism and God's word. He did this to present her to himself as a glorious church without a spot or wrinkle or any other blemish. Instead, she will be holy and without fault. In the same way, husbands ought to love their wives as they love their own bodies. For a man is actually loving himself when he loves his wife.

At first glance it seems that the wives may be getting the raw end of this deal. And for some people, any number of subsequent glances will yield the same result. If we dwell only on the submission part, it does indeed seem that women might be relegated to inferior status within the relationship. But taken in the context of the entire passage, we see that submission is supposed to be mutual (v. 21).

Who's the boss: the husband or the wife? It's a trick question.

Jesus is the boss. And because He is, both husband and wife are supposed to demonstrate submission to one another, as should any other pair of believers on the planet. If it gets to the point where a family conflict has to go one way or another, the wife is asked to submit. Of course, this is supposedly after the husband has already showered his beloved spouse with large doses of Christlike love, devotion, sacrifice, and commitment.

For any organization to succeed—whether military, business, family, or whatever—someone has to be in charge. Private Hotshot can join the army as a new recruit with an IQ of 210, four doctoral degrees, a bank account in the billions, a black belt in karate, and the world's strongest desire to serve his country. Will he go straight to the head of the Pentagon? Not likely. He will do pushups for Corporal Hillbilly, clean latrines for Sergeant Loudmouth, peel potatoes for Lieutenant Dimwit, and do every sweaty exercise and dirty errand demanded of him by any number of other bosses. In order for the military to function effectively, privates report (submit) to other ranks. Yet this fact says nothing about Private Hotshot's significance as a person. And if his so-called superiors are smart, they will quickly promote him up the ranks to capitalize on his wealth of talent and abilities.

Similarly, in a marriage, the expectation of a wife to submit to the husband has nothing to do with the spiritual qualifications of the wife. The headship of the husband was designed to bring order to the family, the church, and society as a whole. While many people today rankle at this concept, many others see this structure as an ongoing biblical mandate.

Stained-Glass Ceilings?

Moving from the wife's relationship to her husband, let's go to the woman's relationship to the church. Again, the oft-cited passage is frequently a sore point: "Women should be silent during the church meetings. It is not proper for them to speak. They should be submissive, just as the law says. If they have any questions to ask, let them

TRIVIA TIDBIT

Times were changing for women as the New Testament was being written. In Greek culture, women remained extremely secluded, veiled, and weren't allowed to converse with men. Greek women are thought to have been depressed and spiteful as a whole.

In Roman culture, however, women had much more status and opportunity for variety and social interaction. The early involvement of women in the church reflects the changing times for women of that era, even though contemporary people may still frown on *any* restrictions Scripture places on women.

SAYS WHO?

"Supreme authority in both church and home has been divinely vested in the male as the representative of Christ, who is Head of the church. It is in willing submission rather than grudging capitulation that the woman in the church (whether married or single) and the wife in the home find their fulfillment."
—*Elisabeth Elliot*

173

QUESTIONS?

Did the prohibition against women speaking in church equate to a broad, "keep your trap shut" command like some people suggest?

Scripture should always be read in context. The command for females to cover their heads, for example, was in reference to times "if she prays or prophesies" (1 Corinthians 11:5). So women were definitely involved in what was going on during the church services and not forced to sit completely closed-mouthed and shunned. But when certain women (or men, for that matter) are interrupting the entire church service with trivial questions or unnecessary conversation, the instructions for them to not speak are helpful for the good of the church as a whole.

ask their husbands at home, for it is improper for women to speak in church meetings" (1 Corinthians 14:34-35). Furthermore, custom required women to cover their heads during worship, while men had no such restrictions (1 Corinthians 11:4-10).

Commands such as this seem quite harsh to many modern women. Yet we need to remember that women were at least permitted inside the Christian church to participate in the services and sacraments. That in itself was progress for the female gender of the time. (In the temple, women were prohibited from being in the main area where the men worshiped.) The first-century church showed a great deal of respect to women.

The question is whether or not all these biblical mandates are still expected of 21st-century women. A few churches still demand head coverings for women. Many more are resistant to allowing women to hold any kind of authoritative position. And they point directly to Scripture to back their policies.

On the other hand, these aren't the *only* references to women in Scripture. Some churches encourage women to identify and apply their spiritual gifts at any and all levels, defending such a tolerant policy because the Bible actually speaks quite highly of women.

While few serious religious leaders during New Testament times would even speak to women on the street, Jesus seemed to go out of His way to include them in His ministry. He initiated a conversation with the woman at the well (John 4). He didn't condemn the woman caught in the act of adultery (John 8:1-11). Scripture gives much attention to Elizabeth (His relative), Mary (Jesus' mother), Anna (the priestess who saw Jesus in the temple as a baby), Mary Magdalene, sisters Mary and Martha, and others. Their stories teach us valuable spiritual truths.

Jesus healed women as well as men. Women followed the disciples as they ministered. And to the discomfort of the men around Him, Jesus even allowed women to anoint Him with perfume and wash His feet (with tears, no less) on occasion (Luke 7:36-50; John 12:1-8). Women were at the crucifixion, and first at the tomb to hear of the resurrection.

As the church was just forming, women remained prominent.

Philip the deacon/evangelist had four virgin daughters who were prophetesses (Acts 21:8-9). The first European converts were women (Acts 16:13-15). In Paul's letters, he singles out women for special greetings, some of whom are identified as church officials (Romans 16:1-3, 6, 14-15, etc.).

Even tucked away in the Old Testament are glorious stories of strong and courageous women: Deborah, Ruth, Esther, Miriam, Sarah, Rachel, and others. Another less familiar story is telling as well. In the days of Moses, when women had few rights in comparison to men, a man named Zelophehad had five daughters and no sons. The rule was that property was passed along to sons, and when Dad died, these five sisters had no legal right to inherit anything. They brought their situation to the attention of Moses and the other leaders, who in turn asked God what to do about it. God's response was logical: give the daughters of Zelophehad the land that had belonged to their father. Because they questioned the tradition of the time, a new law was established that gave women additional rights. (See Numbers 27:1-11.)

Some Christians feel that when women get this much ink in Scripture amid a culture that didn't do much to build their self-esteem, it demonstrates that women have great value and worth that ought not be subdued. The submission passages are still there as well and need to be addressed. Yet given the totality of the information about women, some Christian churches feel the freedom to allow them to get involved at every level the men do.

Bringing order to a church body requires a great deal of discipline, and all the rules can get cumbersome—especially if one entire gender feels slighted. Whether or not limits are imposed on women's participation, and in spite of any other problems faced between the genders today, we need to remember that these are temporary, human constraints. God never sees one gender, race, or social status as any more or less important than another. For now, the best the church can do is attempt to interpret Scripture to the best of its ability and apply all discovered truth to its regular worship activities. If something seems unfair now, God will certainly make everything right and equal in His perfect kingdom.

SAYS WHO?

"A woman's preaching is like a dog's walking on his hinder legs. It is not done well; but you are surprised to find it done at all."—*Samuel Johnson*

SAYS WHO?

"The Bible and Church have been the greatest stumbling blocks in the way of woman's emancipation." —*Elizabeth Cady Stanton*

"All who have been united with Christ in baptism have been made like him. There is no longer Jew or Gentile, slave or free, male or female. For you are all Christians—you are one in Christ Jesus" (Galatians 3:27-28).

Just as women have had to struggle for equality in society during the past century and are still not quite where they would like to be, so they may need to continue to persevere in the church. But anyone who uses a spiritual gift on behalf of the church body in selflessness and humility will be rewarded by God, if not immediately respected by his or her peers. The church owes much to its faithful women throughout the centuries—past and present.

Homosexuality: Out of the Closet and into the Church?

And in spite of the disagreements pertaining to male/female relationships within Christianity, perhaps an even bigger concern these days is homosexuality. To what extent should the church accommodate homosexuals who want to get involved? Some churches welcome homosexual couples and even perform "holy union" ceremonies, since most states don't allow legal gay marriages. Other churches organize protests against homosexuality with a fervor that makes the Salem witch trials seem like a tea party in contrast.

This issue is causing many in the church to reevaluate long-standing positions. Many denominations are convening to discuss the matter and determine how they wish to respond. Some are dividing based on diverse wishes of its member churches. Other scattered congregations are withdrawing from denominations in order to practice as they wish.

The traditional church stance has been that homosexuality is clearly sinful, and therefore not allowed in a church setting, of all places. The first verse we tend to hear from conservative spokespeople is Leviticus 18:22: "Do not lie with a man as one lies with a woman; that is detestable" (NIV). The newer translations read, "Do not practice homosexuality; it is a detestable sin" (NLT). And the consequences of choosing such a lifestyle were spelled out just as clearly: "The penalty for homosexual acts is death to both parties. They have committed a detestable act and are guilty of a capital offense" (Leviticus 20:13).

In response, some people are quick to point out that Leviticus also contains a number of other "outdated" laws and rules. When was the last time we saw a child stoned to death for swearing at a parent (Leviticus 20:9)? When was the last time you had a priest over to check out the house after a bad case of mildew or to regulate the healing of a nasty skin lesion (Leviticus 13:18-23; 47-59)? Our dietary restrictions aren't nearly so stringent as they used to be (Leviticus 11). And some say that the prohibition against homosexuality is just as "outdated" as those other Old Testament laws.

Not so, rebuts the conservative element. While a number of things changed as we went from Old Testament law to New Testament grace, the fact that homosexuality remains a no-no continues throughout the New Testament. Two emphatic passages are Romans 1:26-27 and 1 Corinthians 6:9-10.

It seems clear enough, say some people, that until homosexuals are willing to "straighten up," the church cannot in good conscience allow them to fully participate. As with most other issues, of course, the lines are drawn in different places. A number of conservative churches encourage attendance and participation of anyone and everyone, yet will be much more restrictive when it comes to church leadership. Homosexuals will eventually be expected to renounce their lifestyle or at least cease active practice. The same demands would be placed on adulterers, alcoholics, and others who continued to exhibit what the Bible defines as sinful activity.

Other churches place no such restrictions on practicing homosexuals, including them in leadership and even performing official ceremonies to unite them as couples. And yet these churches also feel they conform to biblical teachings.

Their argument is that homosexuality is not merely a personal choice but a predetermined natural design. Just as some people are born with heterosexual biological urges, so they say, others have homosexual passions instead. Even if some of us believe such feelings are genetically incorrect, they must be God-given. And if this large group of people has no choice in the matter, to deny them full participation in the church is wrong. Just as Jesus gave full respect to lepers, women, Samaritans, and other persecuted minorities of

SEE FOR YOURSELF

In a section about people who have rejected God, Paul writes: "That is why God abandoned them to their shameful desires. Even the women turned against the natural way to have sex and instead indulged in sex with each other. And the men, instead of having normal sexual relationships with women, burned with lust for each other. Men did shameful things with other men and, as a result, suffered within themselves the penalty they so richly deserved" (Romans 1:26-27).

TRIVIA TIDBIT

Don't look for the word *homosexual* in the King James Version of the Bible. The translation says instead that anyone who is "effeminate" will not enter the kingdom of God. Ironically, history tells us that King James himself was . . . uh . . . effeminate.

TRIVIA TIDBIT

As of this writing, long-standing world-wide resistance to homosexual marriage seems to be crumbling. Legal gay marriages are now conducted in Canada, the Netherlands, and the state of Vermont, among other places. The Netherlands has eliminated all references to gender in laws regarding marriage and adoption.

His day, so the church needs to reach out in acceptance of the increasingly active homosexual community.

The confusion is likely to continue for a while as both scientists and theologians debate the nature, and even the definition, of homosexuality. Opinions remain strongly divided. It's easy for those within the church to perceive most homosexuals to be of the "flaming" variety, with promiscuous sexual habits and outrageous lifestyles. But it's much harder to explain why a heterosexual philanderer who regularly harbors lust in his heart is more welcome in most churches than a loving, committed, monogamous gay couple.

Pride Is a Problem—Gay or Straight

And in spite of any official church policy, either involving homosexuality or not, it may be that some churches tend to discriminate against homosexuals without realizing it. If we look at the New Testament command against homosexuality in its context, we see a number of other sins listed that the church tends to tolerate much more readily: "Those who indulge in sexual sin, who are idol worshipers, adulterers, male prostitutes, homosexuals, thieves, greedy people, drunkards, abusers, and swindlers—none of these will have a share in the kingdom of God. There was a time when some of you were just like that, but now your sins have been washed away, and you have been set apart for God" (1 Corinthians 6:9-11).

Many churches sponsor AA meetings to help "drunkards." They work with abusers and adulterers. And what Sunday morning church service is without its fair share of thieves, greedy people, and swindlers? Yet some churches may tend to place more emphasis on the wrongness of homosexuality above any of these other things.

Even the Old Testament refuses to isolate homosexuality as a sin more or less abominable than any other. The twin cities of gay pride in the Old Testament were Sodom and Gomorrah, and staunch conservatives frequently like to point to their fire-and-brimstone destruction (Genesis 19) to show what God thinks of homosexuality. But again, if we put the story into context and read the rest of the Bible, we may see the account in a different light.

Centuries later, after Israel and Judah had been taken into captivity because of idolatry and other major sins against God, the Lord sent a message to them through Ezekiel the prophet:

> "As surely as I live, says the Sovereign Lord, Sodom and her daughters were never as wicked as you and your daughters. Sodom's sins were pride, laziness, and gluttony, while the poor and needy suffered outside her door. She was proud and did loathsome things, so I wiped her out, as you have seen. . . . In your proud days you held Sodom in contempt. But now your greater wickedness has been exposed to all the world, and you are the one who is scorned" (Ezekiel 16:48-50, 56-57).

Indeed, homosexuality typified by rape, abuse, and perhaps even murder was rampant in Sodom and Gomorrah. And this is how we tend to remember those Old Testament cities. But it wasn't *just* the homosexuality that was recalled by Ezekiel but the more basic problems of pride, sloth, and gluttony. And according to God, later generations of those who called themselves by His name were guilty of "greater wickedness." The gay pride of Sodom and Gomorrah paled in comparison to the spiritual pride of God's people during Ezekiel's day. Can Christians today say we're doing any better?

While believers may legitimately use Scripture to justify a stand against homosexuality, many need to seek a broader and deeper understanding of what the Bible has to say about sin in general. So do those who attempt to chide the church into justifying the blind acceptance of homosexuals regardless of their attitudes, practices, and spiritual condition.

Regardless of the tolerance levels of individuals or church boards, it would seem that at the very least, from a biblical perspective, homosexuality is included in the list of behaviors that should be abandoned by those who wish to pursue greater devotion to God in a church setting. Scripture doesn't endorse anything-goes homosexual practice within church walls, nor does it justify the other extreme of homophobia.

QUESTIONS?

Can homosexuals choose to become straight if they really want to?

If you're looking for a *scientific* answer to this question, the jury is still out. Certain Christian groups have formed with the purpose of "converting" homosexuals and restoring them to heterosexuality. The goal of such "reparative therapy" is to achieve, if not a complete change to heterosexuality, at least an abstinence from homosexual acts. The American Psychiatric Association has gone on record against such therapy, citing potential dangers of depression, anxiety, and self-destructive behavior. Yet other reputable studies have suggested that sufficiently motivated homosexuals can change if they really want to.

SAYS WHO?

"The orgasm has replaced the Cross as the focus of longing and the image of fulfillment."—*Malcolm Muggeridge*

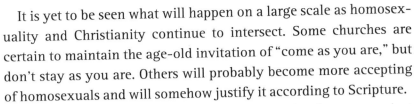

"In necessary things, unity; in doubtful things, liberty; in all things, charity."
—*Richard Baxter*

Gamaliel's advice to his peers might apply to us as well:
    "So my advice is, leave these men alone. If they are teaching and doing these things merely on their own, it will soon be overthrown. But if it is of God, you will not be able to stop them. You may even find yourselves fighting against God" (Acts 5:38-39).

It is yet to be seen what will happen on a large scale as homosexuality and Christianity continue to intersect. Some churches are certain to maintain the age-old invitation of "come as you are," but don't stay as you are. Others will probably become more accepting of homosexuals and will somehow justify it according to Scripture.

Not so many decades ago the church took a hard stance against divorced people in leadership roles. A few still do. Concerned Christians could point to clear biblical passages to remind us that God hates divorce (Malachi 2:16) and that any church leader should be the husband of one wife (1 Timothy 3:2). But as more and more pastors and church leaders got divorced and remarried, gradually the stigma of divorce faded away in many churches. While remaining a tragic statistic in the eyes of most, divorced people eventually found inclusion in the same churches that once excluded them. Will the same be true of homosexuality? We will have to wait and see.

So What Do *You* Think?

In the meantime we need to turn our attention from "what Christians believe" to "what I believe." As we have seen in this and the previous three chapters, we have a bit of leeway in regard to what we think about many of these topics. Certain teachings remain black and white, but many others have a few shades of gray. When the Bible leaves a bit of freedom, we must be careful not to abuse it. In choosing to believe and worship as we do, we need to remember that not everyone is likely to reach the exact same conclusions. As we enjoy our freedom to worship as we wish, we have to extend the same right to others.

The church has been dealing with dissension and diverse opinions for centuries, and nothing is likely to change in the near future. But history provides us a look at some mistakes others made that we might be able to avoid with a bit of wisdom and sensitivity. Can we learn to stand firm in our faith without unnecessarily trashing someone else's? Can we demonstrate the love of Jesus for all other humans—even those who are currently involved in lifestyles we don't approve of? And can we be sensitive to other viewpoints without losing our personal convictions and understanding of the truth?

It's a delicate balance, to be sure. We might do well to review the outlook of Paul's teacher, Gamaliel. When Christianity was first coming onto the scene and threatening to divide the Jewish community, many of the religious leaders wanted to execute those involved in the "new" religion. But Gamaliel reminded them of previous leaders who had gathered a lot of followers, yet came to nothing, given time. His advice for his peers was to cool it for a while and let God act if He wanted to. Until we're absolutely sure which side God is on in any struggle, we do well not to expend a lot of energy on our own. It might just be wasted effort.

Other religions will continue to exist. No matter what we do, certain sects within the Christian church will sometimes misinterpret Scripture and deceive people. Homosexuality isn't going to go away just because many in the church oppose it. Even if Roe vs. Wade is overturned one day, abortion won't disappear just because it becomes illegal. No one is ever likely to find enough evidence to convince scientific minds of the credibility of creation rather than evolution.

The church will always be faced with these issues, and probably more severe problems in the future. We can try to get out there and teach the world to sing in perfect harmony, but it isn't likely to happen. So it's important to establish personal convictions and core beliefs. Otherwise, we tend to become the kind of people James wrote about: "doubtful minded" and "as unsettled as a wave of the sea that is driven and tossed by the wind" (James 1:6).

All Christians don't always believe the same things, but it's important to believe *something*. Do your homework. Read. Pray. Discuss. Ponder. God never promises us all the answers, but He does promise wisdom and His continual attention.

And while you're getting smarter and stronger (from a spiritual perspective, at least), try to remember that others aren't yet where you are. As you personally thrust your roots deeper into the truths you discover, you can also practice showing patience and tolerance for others. That will be the theme of our final chapter.

SAYS WHO?

"We know too much and are convinced of too little."—*T. S. Eliot*

Questions to Ponder and/or Discuss

1. What have been your personal experiences, if any, with women's involvement in the church? Do you sense any frustrations from women you know because they can't be as involved as they wish? Or do you think things in your local congregation are as equal as they can possibly be?

2. Determine to what extent you agree with each of the following statements. (1 = Don't agree at all; 5 = No opinion; 10 = Total agreement)

I have a certain amount   1 2 3 4 5 6 7 8 9 10
of fear of homosexuals.

Homosexuality is a sin.   1 2 3 4 5 6 7 8 9 10

Homosexuality is worse   1 2 3 4 5 6 7 8 9 10
than many other sins.

People are homosexuals   1 2 3 4 5 6 7 8 9 10
from birth.

A homosexual can go   1 2 3 4 5 6 7 8 9 10
straight if he or she really
wants to.

Practicing homosexuals   1 2 3 4 5 6 7 8 9 10
should be included in
church fellowship.

Non-practicing   1 2 3 4 5 6 7 8 9 10
homosexuals should be
included in church fellowship.

Every church needs a
clear policy regarding
its stand on homosexuality.
    1 2 3 4 5 6 7 8 9 10

Every church needs a clear policy regarding its stand on homosexuality.	1 2 3 4 5 6 7 8 9 10
In most cases, "Don't ask, don't tell" is a good policy.	1 2 3 4 5 6 7 8 9 10

3. Do you know anyone who has strongly different opinions on homosexuality and/or women in the church with whom you could have an in-depth conversation in the near future? What questions might you want to ask? What questions might you be asked that you would have the most problem answering?

PART FOUR

Epilogue

CHAPTER SIXTEEN

One Church, Under God?

Unity in the 21st-Century Church

A couple of decades before the W.W.J.D. ("What Would Jesus Do?") phenomenon hit the Christian bookstores, you used to see people wearing pins that read "PBPGIFWMY." If anyone was curious enough to ask, the wearer would explain that it stood for, "Please be patient. God isn't finished with me yet."

Maybe it's time to print PBPGIFWMY on large banners and post the reminder prominently in every *church*. What started as a selfless and coherent body that endured the worst of persecution and accomplished the best of results for their Lord has become a plethora of denominations and congregations that seem to present little if any unity from the viewpoint of the non-believing world. As you've probably noticed while going through this book (and if you're still reading, give yourself a pat on the back), it's not always easy to define exactly "what Christians believe."

If we look at history one way, it doesn't seem that the church has done much right since the first century. As persecution drove believers away from the safety and security of Jerusalem, the

187

SAYS WHO?

"No kingdom has ever had as many civil wars as the kingdom of Christ."
—*Baron de Montesquieu*

church went from being a single "universal" church into a vast variety of names, denominations, worship styles, and more. What one group of believers believed weren't necessarily the same beliefs that other believers believed.

But looking at history from another perspective, we see that the church is still around and in relatively good health. How many other organizations can say the same after two thousand years? Jesus built the church on a rock, as we have seen, so it was meant to last. The first-century and twenty-first-century versions of the church may have precious few similarities, but one fact remains: While we may not be united in our opinions about every single doctrine, we remain united as believers. You may not agree with that other denomination across the street about how to worship, when to worship, what to expect in the end times, or any number of other specifics. But if both you and that group of people have placed your faith in Jesus for your ultimate salvation, you share an eternal connectedness.

It's now time for us to improve that connectedness as much as we can. In our shortsighted thinking, we may come to believe the battle lines are drawn between Protestant and Catholic, Baptist and Church of Christ, Lutheran and Pentecostal, Methodist and Mennonite. Wrong! Nor are the battle lines formed between Christians and non-Christians. (How quickly we tend to forget that we all start as non-Christians!) Rather, the battle lines are drawn between God and Satan, Christians and forces of evil. Satan's army is united and looking for victims. Isn't it a shame that God's army is using so much ammunition to face off and shoot *at each other*?

What the World Needs Now

Now, more than ever, Christians need to regenerate a sense of unity between us. People outside the church are looking for help and direction, yet their perception of a weak or bickering church is not appealing. Indeed, the recent trend for those curious about God has been to explore "spirituality" rather than "religion." Seekers are

drifting through religious organizations like grazing at an expansive buffet in a restaurant, picking out an eclectic assortment of tidbits that appeal to them: a little Christianity, a bit of Buddhism, some Hindu here and there, assorted New Age appetizers, and anything else that appears tasty.

But create-your-own-theology strategies do not provide satisfying answers to the questions of life. That's why this book has dealt with doctrine rather than merely "feel good" passages of Scripture. It's not always fun to pay serious attention to the more complicated portions of the Bible when we see others examining their *chakras*, conducting fire walks, zoning out in front of burning incense or bubbling fountains, and doing other mystic and mysterious things. Yet Bible study leads us to truth, which helps us establish doctrine. And in truly turbulent times, that solid understanding of truth will be far more helpful than any other option available to us.

If only seekers could get a glimpse of "the church" as it was created to be! If the church operates as a body of believers united under the headship of Jesus, it can then pass along the love, care, and tenderness that only Jesus has to offer. But if the outside world sees "the churches" as an endless array of congregations, each with its own unique sales patter like barkers outside carnival freak shows, it's easier to maintain a pick-and-choose mentality rather than committing to a single church body.

So a case can be made for much greater unity between denominations. If the new family in the neighborhood chooses First Presbyterian over First Wesleyan, so be it. Let the Wesleyans swallow hard and attempt to enlist the next new family in town. But only as we perceive ourselves to truly be "the church" rather than "the churches" will the cause of Christ be fulfilled.

But these days it's not just seekers who do the church pew shuffle. It has become much too common for believers to flit from one church to another, assessing every minor aspect like Goldilocks breezing through the home of the Three Bears. ("These seats are too hard." "This carpet is too red." "This method of baptism is too wet." "The bagels were better where we went last week.") Some churches are overly eager to accommodate potential new members, so it's a

SAYS WHO?

"Tolerance implies no lack of commitment to one's own beliefs. Rather it condemns the oppression or persecution of others."—*John F. Kennedy*

TRIVIA TIDBIT

A recent CNN/*USA Today*/Gallup poll showed that 75 percent of Americans do not view their religion as the only true path to God. More than 80 percent of that group believed that another path to God was equally as good as their own.

SEE FOR YOURSELF

"Remind everyone of these things, and command them in God's name to stop fighting over words. Such arguments are useless, and they can ruin those who hear them. Work hard so God can approve you. Be a good worker, one who does not need to be ashamed and who correctly explains the word of truth. Avoid godless, foolish discussions that lead to more and more ungodliness. This kind of talk spreads like cancer" (2 Timothy 2:14-17).

buyer's market for visitors. The downside is that it's just as easy for many of those people to decide to leave as quickly as they decided to stay.

Why Don't You Stay, Just a Little Bit Longer?

According to the Bible, certain things should rarely, if ever, create division among its members. But to be truthful, in this day and age they are the very things that cause a lot of us to seek new and different church homes. Below are a few of the things on the list.

Conflict over personal preference of pastor (1 Corinthians 1:10-17)

The early church argued over who was the best leader: Paul, Peter, Apollos, or someone else. And, of course, there was the group that always seems to be around saying, "*We* follow Jesus. Nyah, nyah, nyah!" Paul pleaded with his readers to establish harmony, reduce divisions, and quit trying "to divide Christ into pieces."

It's good advice for today's church, as well. So what if your guy doesn't have a television ministry and their guy does? So what if their guy tells better jokes than your guy? So what if their guy has 100 times as many in his church than your guy? So what if their guy isn't even a guy, but a popular speaker of the female persuasion?

Why do we need to bicker and goad one another about such things? As long as our leaders are responding to God's call in their lives and speaking God's truth from the pulpit, can't we offer our faithful support?

Taking petty personal problems to church with you (Philippians 4:2-3)

When writing the church at Philippi, Paul singled out two women named Euodia and Syntyche. He pleaded with them to "settle your disagreement." But these weren't just a couple of rowdies off the street; they had already established a good reputation for working hard with Paul and other Christian leaders in "telling others the Good News."

Conflict happens. It always will. And while it is so very easy to change churches (or start your own) every time a personal disagreement arises, the biblical appeal is to unity within church walls and between believers of different churches.

Lawsuits (1 Corinthians 6:1-8)

Apparently a problem in early Corinth was that Christians were taking other Christians to court. Paul was quick to point out the irony: one person who supposedly possessed the insight and wisdom of God was suing another person who supposedly possessed the insight and wisdom of God. Yet the two would go before a secular court where the magistrates making the final decisions didn't necessarily possess the insight and wisdom of God. Why in the world would anyone want to settle a dispute that way?

Yet perhaps no society in history is as quick to lay down the lawsuit as ours. And you can be sure that people are watching—just look at the success of the many courtroom TV shows, and there's even a cable channel devoted entirely to real-life courtroom drama. But what do non-believers think when they see a lot of Christians suing each other? ("Well, your honor, he knocked my Bible on the ground and it got quite dirty. He offered to buy me a new one, but it was my good Bible with all my favorite passages underlined about loving other people. So I don't just want a new Bible; I want his house and SUV as well!")

Paul's solution to the lawsuit problem is simple but unpopular: "Why not just accept the injustice and leave it at that? Why not let yourselves be cheated?" If a few more people were willing to take his advice, perhaps the church would be much stronger today.

Competition in regard to spiritual gifts (1 Corinthians 12)

The Holy Spirit, with limitless wisdom and perception, assigns spiritual gifts to all Christians. And rather than giving every single believer the exact same proportions of the same gifts, His master plan is to assign people the gifts they are more suited to, and then they can depend on each other as they accomplish great things for God. However, the church at Corinth was already in heated debate about whose gifts were the best gifts. And those without certain desired gifts were envious of others who had them.

In spite of Paul's lengthy advice, the argument continues to this

SAYS WHO?

"Somebody figured it out—we have 35 million laws trying to enforce Ten Commandments."—*Earl Wilson*

191

QUESTIONS?

What's the difference between a church and a cult?

A cult may look very much like a church, but most cults rely on sources of "new truth" that supplement or replace the Bible. The traditional teachings of Christianity are usually run through some "spin control" in order to allow cult leaders to appear more significant and inspired than they actually are, even though they are often strong and charismatic to begin with. Jesus is not the last word in salvation; the designated leader of the cult has the final say. Cults usually demand much work from their devotees, which is associated with the eventual salvation of the eager-to-please followers.

day. Many Christians don't value their clearly God-given gifts and seek to exchange them for something else, like kids swapping lunches in the school cafeteria. If someone is determined to use her self-proclaimed gift of singing yet is always in the shadow of much better singers in one church, she might go to another church where she can be "up front" more of the time. Perhaps, however, her true spiritual gift is children's ministry, and she would have done wonders with the kids (including children's choir) at her original church. If we find ourselves constantly church-hopping to exercise what we believe to be a spiritual gift, perhaps we need to double check.

Should I Stay or Should I Go?

So in spite of these and numerous other challenges, Christians are encouraged to deal with the problems and establish a higher standard of unity within the church. A greater degree of tolerance, patience, and perseverance among a few members may just make the difference between a church that operates as it should and one that simply goes through the motions.

But having said that, we also need to say that there *are* certain valid reasons for bailing on one church and seeking involvement elsewhere. For one thing, these days we can't even be sure that every organization that calls itself a "church" has anything to do with Christianity. The cult that follows Sun Myung Moon, for example, has taken the name, "The Unification Church." And while "unification" and "church" are two positive words used in many Christian settings, Moon's organization is by no means Christian. Several other so-named "churches" are considered cults as well. A Christian church is built upon the truths of Scripture and the belief that Jesus Christ is both Savior and Lord. The Bible is the sole written authority, salvation is by grace through faith, and the life, death, and resurrection of Jesus have completed God's plan of redemption. Nothing else is needed (other than the decision of the person to receive in faith what God offers).

It's not only cults that get off-track. Sometimes churches become deceived or deceptive. If we find ourselves in one of the following situations, perhaps the best option is to clear out and look elsewhere.

Refusal to hear the truth (Matthew 10:5-15)

From the very first evangelistic mission, Jesus warned His followers that some places simply wouldn't be responsive to their message. His advice was for them to "shake off the dust of that place from your feet as you leave."

If we find ourselves amid groups who make no pretense of believing what the Bible has to say, it's probably best to move on. It may be tempting to try to sway a large crowd to your way of thinking, but it makes little sense logically. Why spend so much effort talking to deaf ears when you can just as easily find a crowd who *does* want to hear what you have to say?

Refusal to hear the *whole* truth (2 Corinthians 11:1-15)

However, it is more likely that we'll run upon groups who aren't willing to pursue the *entire* truth. Many profess to know and adhere to the truth, yet they soon reveal that they have either been deceived or have settled on something that merely passes for truth. Such people frustrated Paul as he chided the Corinthians: "You seem to believe whatever anyone tells you, even if they preach about a different Jesus than the one we preach, or a different Spirit than the one you received, or a different kind of gospel than the one you believed." Tolerance is not an asset if it allows heresy to infiltrate the church.

As believers, we should have some degree of personal experience with God. We may not know a lot of theology. We may not know much about church history or anything officially "religious." But we *should* know from personal experience what God has done for us. And to allow someone else to interfere with God's clear presence in our lives is dangerous. While experienced Christians may be ready to take on other people in logic and debate, young and inexperienced Christians will do well to put distance between themselves and false teachers.

SEE FOR YOURSELF

Jesus practiced what He preached. Once when He and the disciples got the bum's rush from a Samaritan village, the disciples wanted to call down fire from heaven on the snooty city. Jesus rebuked His disciples and simply went to another village (Luke 9:51-56).

SAYS WHO?

"The equal tolerance of all religions . . . is the same thing as atheism."
—*Pope Leo XIII*

193

SAYS WHO?

"We should not permit tolerance to degenerate into indifference."
—*Margaret Chase Smith*

SEE FOR YOURSELF

"We are all one body, we have the same Spirit, and we have all been called to the same glorious future. There is only one Lord, one faith, one baptism, and there is only one God and Father, who is over us all and in us all and living through us all" (Ephesians 4:4–5).

Recurring sins in church that are never addressed (1 Corinthians 5)

Even when truth is being *taught* in church, we must ensure it is being *applied* as well. If the church leadership is continually looking the other way when its members publicly commit grievous sins, something must be done. The preferred response is for the church to deal with the sin, even if the offender is temporarily "excused" from fellowship, as was the case in Corinth. But if the church never addresses the problem, who can blame true believers for searching elsewhere to go beyond lip service to God and get actively involved?

United or Untied?

Ever since the church began, it has had to deal with false doctrines floating through the front door in the mouths of persuasive speakers. If we find ourselves in a church willing to tolerate teachings that are contrary to Christianity, it's probably a case where tolerance isn't the best option. Sometimes we have to take a hard stand on what we believe.

But frankly, that's not *usually* the case. More often than not, it's too *little* tolerance that causes problems, rather than too much. We seem to have forgotten how to "turn the other cheek" (if, indeed, we ever learned how to begin with). If it's not official religious doctrines that divide us these days, it's the fact that somebody didn't speak to us, or left us off a committee, or slighted us in some other small way.

No doubt we will make mistakes along the road to spiritual unity. Everybody else will, too. So let's try not to keep harping on *their* mistakes while overlooking our own. We may err on the side of tolerance while they seem strict and exclusive in contrast. Or perhaps we're the ones who won't back down over an issue of doctrine, and we can't understand how someone else can be so callously tolerant when their faith is at stake. In spite of the differences that continually try to separate believers, we need to work a bit harder than normal to maintain the unity that is possible only through the Spirit of God active in our lives.

Aesop told a story about a frustrated father who had a number of sons who just couldn't get along and who shunned all his attempts to unite them. One day he walked in with a bundle of sticks tied together and challenged each son in turn to try to break it. None could even come close. Then the father untied the bundle and had them break the sticks one by one. No problem! *Snap, snap, snap.* Aesop's point: In union there is strength.

The same point is true of Christianity as well. If the denominations could get along a little better, we would surely be much stronger. But as we have seen in our examination of what Christians believe, another truism is: In unifying, we will face problems.

SEE FOR YOURSELF

"Don't team up with those who are unbelievers. How can goodness be a partner with wickedness? How can light live with darkness? What harmony can there be between Christ and the devil? How can a believer be a partner with an unbeliever? And what union can there be between God's temple and idols? . . . Therefore, come out from them and separate yourselves from them, says the Lord" (2 Corinthians 6:14-17).

Choices for Choosy Church Choosers

So what are our options as we finish reading this book and go out into the real world again? We have relatively few choices when it comes to practicing Christianity. And we can look around at others who have taken those options to see how we might adapt in each case.

Option #1: Isolation

If you really want to practice what you believe and not have to worry about other doctrines or philosophies, you can find a number of like-minded people and establish your own communities. After all, physical separation is the best guarantee of religious separation.

The Amish people are among those who hold to this philosophy. The Bible calls for believers to be separate from the rest of the world. While most denominations teach that this command is primarily a spiritual matter, others respond to it literally—and live quite happily as a result. Recent studies of Amish people have shown that after being raised in the culture, youngsters tend to be satisfied with the lifestyle and show little desire for "outside" life, even though they are frequently portrayed in the media as having strong wanderlust.

Option #2: Power blocs

A second philosophy suggests that as long as you're getting together with people who believe as you do, you may as well try to make your

TRIVIA TIDBIT

We like to think that people who aren't sincere about their faith are a small minority. Yet sadly, polls that evaluate moral/ethical behavior regularly find little statistical difference between those who profess to be Christians and the general public.

SEE FOR YOURSELF

"Therefore, since we are surrounded by such a huge crowd of witnesses to the life of faith, let us strip off every weight that slows us down, especially the sin that so easily hinders our progress. And let us run with endurance the race that God has set before us. We do this by keeping our eyes on Jesus, on whom our faith depends from start to finish" (Hebrews 12:1-2).

presence known. Rather than isolate yourself, go up against the pagan culture head-on. Sway voters and lawmakers to design society as you believe it should be. If a big group has united to leave religion out of the picture, recruit a bigger group and vote it back in.

This option tends to work better, naturally, where there are large groups of believers to draw support from. But with the influx of people practicing other religions, the decline of traditional Christianity overall, and other factors, it's becoming harder for effective Christian power blocs to form and get their way. Yet just because Christians are outnumbered doesn't mean everyone is going to give up. Such a challenge is just what a lot of Christian groups are looking for.

Option #3: Faking it

This option has worked remarkably well for people throughout history. If you have never tried it, you might be surprised how easy it is for someone to profess Christianity and be regularly involved in a church, yet not allow that spiritual commitment to interfere with secular jobs, behavior, or character.

Who would suspect that the angelic teenager in Sunday school was answering to the name "Party Girl" at last night's rave, or that the church chairman is known as a ruthless, immoral boss at work? We all know it shouldn't be done, yet many people choose to lead double lives at church and/or work or school.

Option #4: "Guerilla" spiritual warfare

Other Christians don't believe they should isolate themselves, get involved in boycotts and petitions, or fake it. They want to do more for God, yet are still at a timid, insecure stage of spiritual progress. Such people may run hot-and-cold for a while. If the coast is clear and no one is looking, they will take a bold stand for Christ. Yet if their actions begin to attract attention or possibly opposition, they quickly take to the shadows.

For many Christians, this is a temporary phase. Others, however, find much comfort in this strategy and stick with it. They may even be involved in churches that operate much the same way, with lots of talk about taking action, but little follow-through. Like the plastic varmints in a Whack-a-Mole game, they pop up every once in a while—just long enough to be seen, but hopefully not long enough to be dealt a painful blow. They serve Christ and others in short, intense bursts—Christian soldiers, to be sure, yet guerilla fighters.

Option #5: Marathon runners

Finally, there is the option of complete and total consistency in lifestyle, worship, and doctrine. Like runners in a marathon race, such people/churches are in it for the long haul and won't stop until the race is over. They pace themselves to make regular progress and keep going by remaining focused on the finish line.

This option is a higher goal than many of the others, but if you're up for the challenge there are a number of churches ready to run alongside you. You're not in this race alone.

For the Love of God!

So what's it going to be? Here we are at the end of this *No-Brainer's Guide to What Christians Believe*, and we're leaving you with a lot of leeway about what to believe. After 2,000 years of Christian history, one more book can't really add much to what has already been said and written. Our primary goal has been to raise the big questions and then help you begin to crystallize a few things to better determine what *you* believe. And now that you're within a few pages of wrapping this book up and perhaps moving on to the newest Grisham novel, we want to challenge you to continue your pursuit of spiritual truth—even in the cerebral areas of doctrine and theology.

The diversity of our beliefs and the freedom to worship as we wish are privileges we dare not take for granted. They have been hard-earned by prior generations and still do not exist for everyone on this earth. Sometimes there are good reasons to hold fast to the things we believe, and sometimes there are good reasons to consider what other people have to say. While we may not agree with everything promoted by other denominations, can't we learn something from the holy separation of the Amish, the centuries-old traditions of the Catholics, the fervent intensity of the Pentecostals,

QUESTIONS?

If I want to keep pursuing the things covered in this book, what are my best options?

When it comes to doctrine and church history, every little bit of information helps contribute to your overall understanding, so never forsake your search for the truth. Keep reading the footnotes in your study Bible. Get a good commentary that explains many of the portions of Scripture that remain unclear to you. Talk to lots of other people to hear their opinions and doubts. Bribe your pastor with a latté and piece of pie, and then hit him up with your lingering questions. But do whatever it takes to crystallize in your own mind what is truth, and then devote yourself to applying it to your life.

SEE FOR YOURSELF

"How wonderful it is, how pleasant, when brothers live together in harmony! For harmony is as precious as the fragrant anointing oil that was poured over Aaron's head, that ran down his beard and onto the border of his robe. Harmony is as refreshing as the dew from Mount Hermon that falls on the mountains of Zion. And the Lord has pronounced his blessing, even life forevermore" (Psalm 133).

the spontaneity of the hip new community church, and many other groups?

Perhaps we need not erect unscalable walls between ourselves and every other group with one or two differences. Like the story of the blind men and the elephant that we mentioned in chapter 1, maybe we're all simply focused on a different aspect of the same God. If we can forego our arguing for a bit, perhaps we can still learn something about Him.

But for those times when you just can't seem to get along with other believers, we leave you with one clear promise:

> "Can anything ever separate us from Christ's love? . . . I am convinced that nothing can ever separate us from his love. Death can't, and life can't. The angels can't, and the demons can't. Our fears for today, our worries about tomorrow, and even the powers of hell can't keep God's love away. Whether we are high above the sky or in the deepest ocean, nothing in all creation will ever be able to separate us from the love of God that is revealed in Christ Jesus our Lord" (Romans 8:35, 38-39).

So for the love of God, cling fast to what you believe as a Christian. If you can also show some love for others who believe different things, fine. If not, just don't let go of your commitment to Jesus. Meanwhile, those other people who don't agree with you can also hold fast to their faith in Jesus. And since nothing can possibly separate you—or them—from Jesus' love, Jesus will hold us together as His church. Whether or not we ever learn to bond as we ought to here and now, we can work out all those pesky disagreements in eternity.

We may see lots of churches. Jesus sees only one. And may we all see more clearly the potential of what might happen as we continue to put our complete trust in Him as the original and ultimate source of what Christians believe.

Questions to Ponder and/or Discuss

1. What would you say is the most interesting thing you learned or the most surprising observation you made while reading this book?

2. What questions still remain for you in regard to what Christians believe? What can you do to continue learning in the weeks and months to come?

3. What grade would you give yourself in the category of tolerance? In what ways have you shown tolerance for others during the past week? Can you think of any examples of intolerance?

You Better Believe It!

Angels

"The angels are the dispensers and administrators of the divine beneficence toward us; they regard our safety, undertake our defense, direct our ways, and exercise a constant solicitude that no evil befall us."—*John Calvin*

Atonement

"When Jesus Christ shed his blood on the cross, it was not the blood of a martyr or the blood of one man for another; it was the blood of God poured out to redeem the world."—*Oswald Chambers*

Baptism

"Baptism points back to the work of God, and forward to the life of faith."—*J. Alice Motyer*

The Bible

"God the Father is the giver of the Holy Scripture, God the Son is the theme of Holy Scripture, and God the Spirit is the author, authenticator, and interpreter of Holy Scripture."—*J. I. Packer*

Born Again

"The first time we're born, as children, human life is given to us; and when we accept Jesus as our Savior, it's a new life. That's what 'born again' means."—*Jimmy Carter*

The Christian Life

"The Christian is not one who has gone all the way with Christ. None of us has. The Christian is one who has found the right road."—*Charles L. Allen*

Christianity

"Christianity is not devotion to work, or to a cause, or a doctrine, but devotion to a person, the Lord Jesus Christ."
—*Oswald Chambers*

The Church

"God never intended his church to be a refrigerator in which to preserve perishable piety. He intended it to be an incubator in which to hatch converts."—*F. Lincicome*

Creation

"Everything is a thought of [an] infinite God and in studying the movements of the solar system, or the composition of an ultimate cell arrested in a crystal, developed in a plant; in tracing the grains of phosphorus in the brain of a man; or in the powers, and actions thereof—I am studying the thought of the infinite God."
—*Theodore Parker*

Crucifixion

"Christ in his weakest hour performed his greatest work, dying on the cross to redeem mankind."—*Anonymous*

Death

"One short sleep past, we wake eternally, and death shall be no more: death, thou shalt die."—*John Donne*

The Devil

"I believe in the devil for three reasons:
1. The Bible plainly says he exists.
2. I see his work everywhere.
3. Great scholars have recognized his existence."—*Billy Graham*

Discipleship

"Discipleship means discipline. The disciple is one who has come with his ignorance, superstition, and sin to find learning, truth, and forgiveness from the Savior. Without discipline we are not disciples."—*Victor Raymond Edman*

Election

"God did not choose us because we were worthy, but by choosing us he makes us worthy."—*Thomas Watson*

Eternity

"This was the strength of the first Christians, that they lived not in one world only, but in two, and found in consequence not tension alone, but power, the vision of a world unshaken and unshakable."—*Harry Emerson Fosdick*

Evangelism

"The Christian is called upon to be the partner of God in the work of the conversion of men."—*William F. Buckley*

Evolution

"That the universe was formed by a fortuitous concourse of atoms, I will no more believe than that the accidental jumbling of the alphabet would fall into a most ingenious treatise of philosophers."—*Jonathan Swift*

Faith

"Faith is a reasoning trust, a trust which reckons thoughtfully and confidently upon the trustworthiness of God."—*John R. W. Stott*

God

"God is the great reality. His resources are available and endless. His promises are real and glorious, beyond our wildest dreams."—*J. B. Phillips*

Gospel

"We can learn nothing of the gospel except by feeling its truths. There are some sciences that may be learned by the head, but the science of Christ crucified can only be learned by the heart."
—*Charles Haddon Spurgeon*

Grace

"The law tells me how crooked I am. Grace comes along and straightens me out."—*Dwight L. Moody*

Heaven

"Heaven is the perfectly ordered and harmonious enjoyment of God and of one another in God."—*St. Augustine*

Hell

"The essence of hell is complete separation from God, and that is ultimate disaster."—*W. R. Mathews*

Holiness

"The essence of holiness is conformity to the nature and will of God."—*Samuel Lucas*

Holy Spirit

"Call the Comforter by the term you think best—Advocate, Helper, Paraclete, the word conveys the indefinable blessedness of his sympathy; an inward invisible kingdom that causes the saint to sing through every night of sorrow. This Holy Comforter represents the ineffable motherhood of God."—*Oswald Chambers*

Humility

"Humility is recognizing that God and others are responsible for the achievements in my life."—*Bill Gothard*

Incarnation

"He clothed himself with our lowliness in order to invest us with his grandeur."—*Richardson Wright*

Jesus Christ

[Jesus said,] "'I am the Way unchangeable; the Truth infallible; the Life everlasting.'"—*Thomas à Kempis*

Justification

"To say that God justifies the ungodly means quite simply that God in his amazing love treats the sinner as if he was a good man. Again, to put it very simply, God loves us, not for anything that we are, but for what he is."—*William Barclay*

Glory of God

"The glory of God, and, as our only means to glorifying him, the salvation of human souls, is the real business of life."—*C. S. Lewis*

Love

"Christian love links love of God and love of neighbor in a two-fold Great Commandment, from which neither element can be dropped, so sin against neighbor through lack of human love is sin against God."—*Georgia Harkness*

Obedience

"Faith and obedience are bound up in the same bundle. He that obeys God, trusts God; and he that trusts God, obeys God."
—*Charles Spurgeon*

Patience

"All comes at the proper time to him who knows how to wait."
—*St. Vincent de Paul*

Praise

"You awaken us to delight in your praise for you have made us for yourself, and our hearts are restless until they rest in you."
—*St. Augustine*

Prayer

"Between the humble and contrite heart and the majesty of heaven, there are no barriers; the only password is prayer."—*Hosea Ballou*

Repentance

"Repentance must be something more than mere remorse for sins; it comprehends a change of nature befitting heaven."
—*Lew Wallace*

Resurrection

"The Gospels do not explain the Resurrection; the Resurrection explains the Gospels. Belief in the Resurrection is not an appendage to the Christian faith; it is the Christian faith."
—*John S. Whale*

Revelation

"God hides nothing. His very work from the beginning is revelation—a casting aside of veil after veil, a showing to men of truth after truth. On and on from fact divine he advances, until at length in his Son, Jesus, he unveils his very face."
—*George MacDonald*

Salvation

"Salvation is moving from living death to deathless life."
—*Jack Odell*

Sanctification

"I cannot crucify my old nature, but Christ can and did."
—*Erwin Lutzer*

Satan

"The devil never sleeps and your flesh is very much alive. Prepare yourself for battle. Surrounding you are enemies that never rest."
—*Thomas à Kempis*

Second Coming

"The primitive church thought more about the Second Coming of Jesus Christ than about death or about heaven. The early Christians were not looking for a cleft in the ground called a grave but for a cleavage in the sky called Glory."
—*Alexander MacLaren*

The Self

"*Flesh* is the Bible's word for unperfected human nature. Leaving off the 'h' and spelling it in reverse we have the word *self*. Flesh is the self-life; it is what we are when we are left to our own devices."—*Billy Graham*

Service

"Dedicate some of your life to others. Your dedication will not be a sacrifice; it will be an exhilarating experience."—*Thomas Dooley*

Sin

"Men never violate the laws of God without suffering the consequence."—*Lydia Maria Child*

Stewardship

"God will not merely judge us on the basis of what we gave but also on the basis of what we did with what we kept for ourselves."
—*Erwin Lutzer*

Suffering

"God is a specialist when the anguish is deep. His ability to heal the soul is profound . . . but only those who rely on his wounded Son will experience relief."—*Charles Swindoll*

Theology

"The Christian faith is the most exciting drama that ever staggered the imagination of man—and the dogma is the drama."—*Dorothy L. Sayers*

The Trinity

"God does not live in isolation—not in the solitude of a single person, but three persons in one essence."—*Lois Evely*

Truth

"If Christ did not speak the truth in all matters, the claims about himself vanish like the idle babbling of a lunatic bent on deceiving the world. Unlike Plato and Aristotle, he could not afford to be wrong—even once."—*Erwin Lutzer*

Worship

"If worship does not change us, it has not been worship. To stand before the Holy One of eternity is to change. Worship begins in holy expectancy; it ends in holy obedience."—*Richard Foster*

Other Tyndale Resources for Further Reading

Here are some additional resources from Tyndale House Publishers that you might want to check out for further information about Christianity and the Bible:

The Bible

The Complete Book of Bible Literacy (Mark D. Taylor)—A broad collection of concise background information to the Bible, such as key Bible people and events, key events in church history, notable quotes about the Bible, and the Bible and the fine arts.

Essential Guide to Bible Versions (Philip W. Comfort)—A textbook and tutorial that answers complex questions about accuracy and translation methods for the many different English Bible translations and that introduces readers to Bible manuscripts and textual criticism.

No-Brainer's Guide to Jesus (James S. Bell and Stan Campbell)—A user-friendly guide to Jesus, beginning with Old Testament prophecies about him and progressing through the Gospels and Paul's letters. It ends with a chapter on Jesus as he is perceived in the 21st century.

No-Brainer's Guide to the Bible (James S. Bell and James Dyet)—A user-friendly guide to the Bible, giving a brief overview of all the major events and topics.

The Origin of the Bible (Philip W. Comfort)—A collection of articles by well-known Bible scholars regarding the inspiration, canon, text, and translations of the Bible.

Quiknotes: English Bible Versions (Philip W. Comfort)—A brief history of English versions of the Bible and short descriptions of the most well-known versions.

Quiknotes: The Books of the Bible (Philip W. Comfort et. al.)—A brief overview of the historical context in which the books of the Bible were written and a short summary of each book's content.

Quiknotes: The Origin of the Bible (Philip W. Comfort)—A brief overview of how the Bible was written and how it has come down to us today.

Tyndale Bible Dictionary (Walter A. Elwell and Philip W. Comfort)—A comprehensive collection of articles that define any significant biblical term or concept.

Tyndale Concise Bible Commentary (Robert B. Hughes and J. Carl Laney)—A single-volume commentary that provides a brief explanation of every passage of the Bible and includes introductions to each Bible book, an article about the theme of the Bible book, and detailed maps of places mentioned in Scripture.

Willmington's Bible Handbook (Harold L. Willmington)—A comprehensive resource providing an explanation of every passage of Scripture, a summary of how each book of the Bible relates to the whole theme of Scripture, an overview of how the Bible was written and passed down to us today, a collection of article about key Bible people, and numerous lists, charts, maps, indexes, and background material.

Willmington's Guide to the Bible (Harold L. Willmington)—A unique combination of a Bible handbook, commentary, topical fact-finder, theological manual, history text, illustrated encyclopedia, cross-reference guide, and archaeological resource.

Theology/Beliefs

Essential Truths of the Christian Faith (R. C. Sproul)—An easy-to-understand introduction to over 100 basic Christian truths. Contains chapter summaries, reading suggestions, and diagrams.

Concise Theology (J. I. Packer)—A brief and easy-to-understand summary of nearly 100 basic Christian beliefs, as explained by one of the premier Reformed theologians of Christianity.

More Than a Carpenter (Josh McDowell)—An apologetic examination of the true nature of Christ and his impact on our lives. Written by a former skeptic of Christianity.

Christianity: The Faith That Makes Sense (Dennis McCallum)—An easy-to-read apologetic that presents a clear, rational defense for Christianity to those unfamiliar with the Bible.

J. I. Packer Answers Questions for Today (J. I. Packer and Wendy Zoba)—A question-and-answer book written by one of the premier Reformed theologians of Christianity.

How Now Shall We Live? (Charles Colson)—A thorough examination of what it means to live and think as Christians, emphasizing the importance of restoring and redeeming every aspect of contemporary culture: family, education, ethics, work, law, politics, science, art, music.

Answers to Tough Questions (Josh McDowell and Don Stewart)—A question-and-answer resource addressing 65 questions about the Bible, God, Jesus Christ, miracles, other religions, and Creation.

Reasons Skeptics Should Consider Christianity (Josh McDowell and Don Stewart)—A question-and-answer resource addressing various questions about the Bible and evolution.

Quiknotes: Christian Classics (Philip W. Comfort and Daniel Partner)—A brief summary of forty-five of the most influential Christian writings (besides the Bible), along with a short biography of each writer.

Now, That's a Good Question! (R. C. Sproul)—A question-and-answer resource that addresses doctrinal points and contemporary issues such as euthanasia, evolution, and abortion.

Christian History

The Story of Christianity (Michael Collins and Matthew Price)—A full-color overview of Christian history, complete with pictures, quotes, and charts.

Who's Who in Christian History (J. D. Douglas and Philip W. Comfort)—A comprehensive list of key figures in Christian history and a brief description about their life and work.

Quiknotes: Christian History (Paul R. Waibel)—A brief overview of Christian history, arranged chronologically and divided into ten chapters, each covering a specific time period.

The Christian Life

No-Brainer's Guide to How Christians Live (James S. Bell and Stan Campbell)—A user-friendly guide to the Christian life, addressing such issues as Bible study, prayer, worship, other spiritual disciplines, the Beatitudes, the fruit of the Spirit, spiritual gifts, the armor of God, marriage, parents and children, friends, work relationships, dealing with those in authority, church relationships, relationships with enemies, self-image, and what God provides for those who seek the Christian life.

Quiknotes: Devotional Classics (Daniel Partner)—A brief summary of thirty-seven devotional classics, along with a brief description

of each author's life. Includes Augustine, Francis of Assisi, John Bunyan, Brother Lawrence, Oswald Chambers, C. S. Lewis, and others.

New Believer's Bible (Greg Laurie)—A complete Bible with notes designed to help new Christians understand and grow in their newfound faith.